THE SECRET OF
SUPERSTITION COVE

A Gideon Ten Adventure

BOOK #2

DEL HAYES

Special thanks to Joshua, Marinda, Micah, and Juda for their inspiration in this writing. Also, special thanks to their friends at church and school for allowing me to "borrow" personalities for my characters.

To Herman, who always makes me laugh,
and to Carolyn, who has inspired me when others could not.

Contents

Chapter One

A Preview of Things to Come

Jim Farmer and Rick Barber sprinted through the hectic airport, dodging passengers, luggage, baby strollers, children who had strayed from their parents, and even terminal employees as they raced to return to their gate. As they sped toward their waiting area the announcement was repeated over the airport's P.A. system, putting them in a state of panic and forcing them to run even faster.

"Attention please! Will Rick Barber and Jim Farmer please report to their departure gate immediately?"

They jumped over benches, spun around chairs, and almost collided with a dog cage, but they kept going. Only three minutes before, they had been at the opposite end of the airport watching the overseas flights arriving, their brief expedition interrupted by the loud speaker announcing the call for Flight 260 to Mexico City.

Ted Simon, Riverside Life Tabernacle's youth minister, had explicitly warned the group to stay together, expressing his fear that someone would miss the flight if they wandered off. Like a self-fulfilling prophesy, two members of the group, known as the Gideon Ten, were discovered to be missing. The group was on their way to help a church in the Yucatan. Their scheduled four-week trip would involve working on the foundation for the new sanctuary before going into the jungle and camping several nights while working with the Mayans.

Ted, who had served as the church's youth pastor for the past six years, was in his late twenties. His dark hair and eyes, contrasted with his wife's light brown hair and ice-water blue eyes. Ted, along with Hector Jiménez, the pastor of the Yucatan church, had been planning the four week trip to the Yucatan for the following summer, however, because of the reward money received by the group for helping to solve a series of robberies that had been plaguing Riverside, the group was able to schedule the trip sooner.

Rick was the group's president, and Jim, his best friend, was the vice president. In spite of Ted's admonition to not wander off, Rick's curiosity overrode all common sense, causing him to grow restless. After sitting for thirty minutes, he grew tired of waiting and thought it would be cool to see as much of the airport as possible. After all, living in Riverside, it wasn't every day that he got the opportunity to explore a large international airport, and even with all the restrictions of Homeland Security there were still many accessible areas that held attractions. They visited several of the stores, even though the prices were more for convenience than practicality and definitely out of their price range. Still, they enjoyed looking at the variety of merchandise available. It was like visiting a mall, only it also had cars and motor-cycles on display.

Jim, unable to bear the thought of Rick roaming loose around the airport by himself, decided to accompany Rick on his trek. They soon lost track of the time. Their journey eventually led them to the far side of the airport where they climbed the observation deck and watched the overseas flights land. Rick was fascinated by the planes that were full of mostly oriental people. He had never seen so many people from places like Japan, Taiwan, China, India, and other countries through-out Asia.

"I wonder what it would be like to be a missionary," Rick said wistfully as he watched the foreigners pass by. "Have you ever thought about it?"

Jim smiled at him. "Rick, did you ever stop to think that's what we're doing on this trip?"

That snapped Rick out of his wanderlust spell. "We need to get back," he said, realizing they had been away too long. Five seconds later the announcement was broadcast to the entire airport.

Rick sidestepped an elderly woman rolling her luggage toward the Delta counter.

"Watch out!" the woman called out.

"Sorry..., excuse me," he hollered over his shoulder as he sped toward his ticket gate. Even though he didn't think she liked his apology very much, he didn't have time to worry about it. His mind was wrestling with the possibility that they had already missed their flight. Upon arriving at the boarding gate, the boys nearly collided with a stern-faced Detective Smallwood of the Riverside Police Department. Detective Smallwood's harsh features appeared even rougher when he was upset, which at the moment appeared to be the case.

"I should have known you two would be getting into something," he said, shaking his head. "I wanted to come down and thank you personally before you left on your trip, but if I hadn't delayed the flight, you wouldn't have a plane to leave on."

"We're sorry," Rick stuttered, "but I wanted..."

"Never mind what you wanted," he said as a hint of a smile formed on his face. "I came to tell you that we've captured all five of the men involved in the theft ring. It would have continued for a long time if your group hadn't gotten involved." His jacket opened enough for Rick to catch a glimpse of the gold badge hooked to his belt.

"Are congratulations in order?" Rick said.

The policeman followed his gaze to the badge. A small smile transformed his plaster-like face, at least a little in Rick's opinion, into that of a human being.

"Well it was coming soon anyway," the police detective said, "but I have a feeling your group sped up the process a little. Also, Sam Upton sends you his regards; he started at the academy yesterday. Anyway, enjoy your vacation; you've earned it. Now get on the plane. I can only hold it for so long before the Air Marshals eventually come out and arrest us all."

They thanked the detective and hurried down the ramp. As they entered the plane, their intent was to go directly to their assigned seats; however, they were immediately spotted and stopped by Ted. His fists were planted firmly on his hips, and the look on his face would have stopped a stampede of frightened cattle. Expecting one of Ted's blood-chilling lectures, the boys were grateful when one of the flight attendants instructed them to move to their seats and buckle in right away.

Jim and Rick knew the reprieve from Ted's wrath was only temporary. They were both aware that he would be waiting for them when they landed, but still, for five hours they planned to enjoy their tiny bit of amnesty. As they hustled down the aisle toward their seats, Jim whispered, "He's pretty mad, Rick. I think we had better cool it when we get to Mexico."

Rick chanced a peek toward the back of their section at Ted who by this time was seated and already fastening his seatbelt. Ted's face was still flushed as he shot darts at the two teens from where he sat in the back with Brenda, his wife.

"I know," Rick answered. If his voice wasn't exactly full of remorse, it *was* slightly contrite. "I was thinking the same thing. All I really wanted to do was just look around a little. I think we should apologize to him as soon as we land."

"Yeah," Jim said, agreeing with his friend. "Also, promise me that we won't get into any trouble while we're in Mexico."

Rick threw his hand over his heart and acted offended.

"Jim," he said, feigning surprise at his friend's lack of trust. "We're going to help a native pastor add a wing onto his church. What kind of trouble could we possibly get into?"

Jim commented that his friend was the worst mime to ever live and started to answer, but the attendant reminded them once again to take their seats as the plane was about to take off.

They had planned to sit together on the plane, Jim on the aisle and Rick by the window, but Wendy and Mackenzie changed places forcing Rick to sit in the middle section with Wendy while Jim sat with Mackenzie.

"You don't mind, do you?" Wendy asked as she playfully entwined her auburn hair around her middle finger.

Rick got lost in the enchanting spell of her green eyes and answered, "No, not at all," even though he secretly had been looking forward to sitting by the window. He wished she had asked him about it first, but he offered her a weak, reassuring smile and said, "Besides, Jim's right across the aisle if I need to talk to him."

Wendy's eyes became mere slits as she gave him a maleficent look. Rick immediately realized he may have said something wrong again, and figured it had something to do with all that Venus and Mars stuff that his Dad had told him about when he had "the talk" with him. His father assured him that he would have the rest of his life to try and figure it all out. Rick guessed that if he ever did, he would be the wisest man to have lived since Jesus. Wendy tossed her hair again and crinkled her nose, giving him a mock pout with her mouth. Rick guessed that she was kidding and not really upset, at least he hoped that was the case. Still, he took it as a warning of something to watch out for in the future.

The flight attendant activated the large movie screen and stood to the side as a small film played explaining to the passengers how to buckle their restraining belts and the use of the air bags and flotation devises in case of an emergency. As the film played, the attendant held up a life jacket as a prop and posed, pointing to the screen like models on *The Price is Right*. Rick was amused by the entire presentation.

"Why do we need flotation devices?" he whispered as he leaned toward Wendy. "We're going to be flying over mountains, not the ocean."

Wendy, still miffed at his previous comment, whispered harshly, "Suppose we crash on a mountain lake."

It came out a little too severe for Rick's comfort. He started to reply but realized that she had him stumped and he didn't want to risk angering her any more than he already had. It was time to cut bait and walk away.

"Well, at least we can use the air bags," he answered. It was a weak comeback, and he knew it, but he still felt better saying it. They put on their seatbelts and adjusted them. He leaned back as the plane began taxiing down the runway. By the time they had lifted off the ground for their five-hour flight, Wendy had gotten over her hurt feelings and they were quickly lost in conversation.

Chapter Two

A Secret Code

Wendy and Rick talked almost continuously or the first hour of the flight. It seemed the most natural thing Rick had ever done. He enjoyed talking with Wendy so much that he forgot all about wanting to sit by the window. He got so lost in conversation with her that he didn't even notice that he had spent very little time talking to Jim.

Jim, on the other hand, seemed to have problems talking one on one with a girl, especially one as attractive as Mackenzie. Though taller and a little older than Rick, and the fact that he had always been full of information and an excellent source of advice where girls were concerned, nevertheless, he found himself tongue-tied when trying to hold his own with one. Rick helped Jim out by throwing a question or two his way so that he and Mackenzie would have something to discuss besides baseball and school.

Wendy had just finished telling Rick about her brother's new truck when Rick helped Jim for the last time. As he turned his attention back to Wendy, she repeated, "As I was saying, Greg bought a new Ford Escape. It's black and reminds me of those government cars they use in the movies."

"Where did he get it?" Rick said.

"He got it at Landers' Ford in Lake Mason."

"That must have been the one I saw at church last Sunday," Rick said. "It still had the dealership's tag on it. That is one sweet ride. I'll bet he loves driving…"

"THAT'S AWESOME!"

Rick turned in his seat to see the source of the disturbance that had erupted behind him. Jim joined him, looking around frantically for the cause of the commotion. The two teens craned their necks to see over the seats, though Rick tried to keep his head down as low as possible, not wishing to attract any unwanted attention from Ted. About seven rows back, four of the group's members were bunched together behind Ken and Kim, staring over their shoulders and laughing. Whatever the two *Braniacs* were up to, they were generating a lot of excitement among the rest of the group and curiosity among the rest of the passengers.

Rick looked at Wendy with an expression that begged a temporary reprieve from their conversation. She nodded to him like a teacher giving permission to a student to go to the restroom, let out a deep breath in exasperation, and said reluctantly, "Go ahead."

Rick and Jim walked to where the group had gathered around the Walker siblings, hoping the commotion would not catch the attention of the flight attendants or receive a reprimand from the Air Marshal.

"Okay," Rick said like a policeman shooing people from the scene of an accident. "What's the fuss all about?"

No one answered, but instead they watched Ken who was holding a sheet of paper and laughing. Craning his neck as far as he could, Rick peeked over Ken's shoulder and saw writing on the paper that appeared to be a cross between Egyptian hieroglyphics and computer codes. Ken handed it to him to look at. Though Jim and Rick studied the paper carefully, they had no clue how to read it. After several minutes they shook their heads and gave the paper back.

"Okay," Rick said. "What is it?"

Ken grinned and said, "It's a secret code. Look at the writing. Do you see any patterns in the symbols?"

Rick and Jim looked at the paper again.

The symbols were:

⟩⊓⌈∨　⌈∨　⌐◻⌊⌊⌊⟨
◻⌊⌐⌐⌊⌈∨⊓　∨⟩⟨⌐⌈⌐

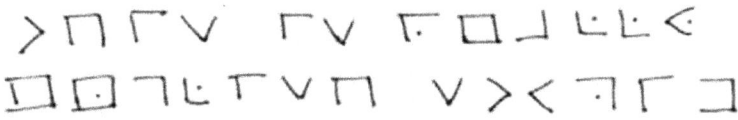

"Not really," Rick said. "I see some symbols repeated, but…, I give up. What do they mean?"

Kim said, "You can read it for yourself. You only need the key."

Rick had grown used to dealing with Ken and Kim through the years. It was almost as if they were constantly speaking Klingon or writing something in hieroglyphics, causing Rick to wonder how many moons they had on their mother planet.

"I'm not as smart as you and Ken," Rick said as he struggled to keep the frustration out of his voice. "There's no way I can know what all these symbols mean. It looks like some sort of computer language…., or is it Mayan?"

"That's the beauty of it. This isn't cuneiform and they're not Mayan symbols either."

Rick felt like an elementary school student sitting through a lecture on astrophysics.

"I still can't read it," he added reluctantly.

"You can read English, can't you?" Ken said. "Letters are nothing more than symbolic representations of actual sounds. For example, the Hawaiian alphabet only has twelve letters in it. Symbols are the basis for written languages worldwide. These symbols aren't any more difficult than our alphabet. Let me show you."

In a matter of seconds Ken wrote down four symbols; two tic-tac-toe grids and two giant exes. Then he placed dots in one of the grids and one of the exes. After that he penciled in the letters of the alphabet and handed it to Rick.

```
A | B | C        J . K | L        W
D | E | F        M . N . O     S/   .
G | H | I        P | Q . R    T X U   X . X . Y
                              / V \    / . \
                                        Z
```

Looking at the key and then back to the message, Rick and Jim grinned at each other. The message read, "THIS IS REALLY ENGLISH, STUPID."

Rick and Jim laughed in spite of being called stupid. The simplicity of the code was amazing, and yet, to someone who wasn't aware of what the symbols represented, it would be almost indiscernible.

"Let me try," Jim said as he grabbed the paper and a pencil. Several seconds later he had written a pun in the new alphabet.

"How else can it be used?" Rick asked.

"Just about any way that a regular alphabet can," Kim answered. "You could write a book or an essay at school, though you wouldn't make any points with your teacher, but on this trip we can use it to pass around secret messages without anyone else knowing about it."

Kim's suggestion about sending secret messages to each other sounded like a colossal idea to Rick. The fact that none of the adults could read them made it even more appealing. He had to admit they did very little of that, but you never knew when the occasion would arise when they would need to send a message that Ted couldn't read. It would be better to have it in advance. Plus, the symbols almost resembled Mayan drawings. They would be perfect for this trip.

Returning to their seats, Jim and Rick shared the new code with Wendy and Mackenzie, and for the remainder of the flight they sent messages back and forth as they discussed topics ranging from music, to Ted and Brenda, the missionary trip they were on, Ted and Brenda, school, oh yes, and Ted without Brenda. Before they knew it, time had flown by and the seatbelt sign came on announcing the plane was preparing to land. The flight attendants announced that they were about to make their final approach and would be on the ground in ten minutes, as they walked throughout the cabin checking to see that everyone was ready for landing.

Wendy couldn't believe the flight was over so soon and said as much to Rick. He said he hoped the rest of the visit didn't fly by as fast, not knowing that before the four weeks were over, he would almost wish for the opposite.

The noisy, busy atmosphere of a major airport can easily be described at any time as hectic and bordering on the edge of chaos, but the Gideon Ten members found Mexico City to be close to the brink of total anarchy compared to the airport they had departed from back home. As they debarked from the plane, their ears were assaulted by blaring announcements over the loud speakers. Adding to the chaos of the foreign language followed by additional announcements in English were ramp attendants barking orders over microphones that in turn were barely heard above the cacophonous volume of hundreds of voices speaking at once. The confusion was made worse by the fact that most of the conversations around them were in Spanish. Upon clearing the ramp, they had to step past the people crowded around the gate, attempting to capture glimpses of loved ones as they disembarked the plane.

Ted was the first of the group to reach an open area, immediately turning around and waiting for Jim and Rick as they exited the flight. His face was a mask of sternness as he watched members of the group come from the tunnel. As they appeared, he pointed to his left, indicating they should go and stand with Brenda. His wait eventually paid off as the last four members appeared. He quickly separated Wendy and Mackenzie from the boys, sending them to his wife while he took Rick and Jim aside.

Not allowing them the opportunity to speak, Ted said, "What

happened back in Ohio will not, I repeat, not reoccur while we're here in Mexico. If it does, I'll put the both of you on the next plane home, and quite frankly, I hope you don't make the connecting flight and end up in Australia or some third world country."

Rick started to say something but was cut off when Ted announced they would not be sitting with the girls for the last leg of their journey.

When they joined the rest of the group, Ted and Brenda quickly organized a new buddy system, being careful not to pair Jim and Rick together. Satisfied that the group was now under control, Ted steered everyone toward the Northeast Wing of the airport and to their next gate. They stopped at two rows of plastic seats near gate seven where Ted had them all sit under the watchful eye of his wife while he went to the airline's counter and inquired about their flight to Mérida.

Rick didn't enjoy being singled out in front of the group or being the inspiration for the new "buddy system," but he had to admit the stunt he and Jim pulled was pretty stupid. Still, if he had to be paired with someone other than Jim or Wendy, at least he and Terrell could talk about baseball, football, and just about any other sport except figure skating which he likened to ballet on ice.

Faced with an hour layover, Ted allowed them to get drinks and refreshments, but gave strict instructions to *everyone* not to leave the area without his knowledge.

When it was finally time to board, they discovered their plane wasn't a large 747 jet like the one they arrived on, but rather an older plane with four propellers. As they walked up the ramp and settled in for the three-hour flight, several of them viewed the plane with skepticism while entering it with an air of caution and trepidation.

After being in the air for thirty minutes, Ted took Rick and Jim aside. "Look, guys. I'm sorry for jumping on you like that, but this trip will be hectic enough without any improvisation on your part. Do you understand what I'm saying?"

"Yes sir," Rick said meekly. "Ted, I want to apologize. It wasn't

Jim's fault. I just wanted to see the airport, and he just..."

"That's not true," Jim interrupted. "I chose to go along with him. He didn't even talk to me about it. I could just as easy have decided not to go."

Ted gave them a genuine smile. "I appreciate the way you two always have each other's back. Well, either way, thanks for making this easier. Would you two like to be paired up again and go sit with the girls?"

Ted and Brenda had been talking about the budding romance between Rick and Wendy, and Jim and Mackenzie. The connection between Rick and Wendy came as no surprise to them, since Rick had been smitten with her for years. They were just amused at the recent development and that Rick had finally started to come out of his shell.

Rick grinned. "Maybe later, but right now I'm playing a baseball trivia game with Terrell, and even though it's his game, I have a seventy-five point lead."

Ted laughed out loud. "I promise I won't tell Wendy about your choice. I have a feeling she would tear into you if she knew she still took second place to baseball. Okay, just remember, this isn't Riverside, and you don't have any mysteries to solve or adventures to experience, and especially, you don't have any police detectives down here to bail you out. This is only a church trip. We're going to help with the building of the new sanctuary, and then we're going to take a camping trip into the interior to work with the Mayans, so just do me a favor and try to stay out of trouble."

They returned to their seats, and by the end of the trip Terrell had passed Rick, leaving Rick to wonder just how important it was to know eight ways a batter could reach first base without getting a hit.

Chapter Three
Pastor Jiménez and Juan

At the airport in Mérida, eleven weary passengers straggled off the plane and waited as Ted located Pastor Jiménez. Ted, on the other hand, seemed to be revived, as he left to search for their host. He took half a dozen steps before stopping as he saw their host approaching.

The man that met them, who everyone assumed was Pastor Jiménez, had the same dark features of his countrymen which was enhanced by his neatly tailored tan suit and cream-colored fedora.

"*Señor Simon*," the man said, "*Soy Hector Jiménez. Bienvenido a México.*"

"*Gracias, Senor Jiménez*," Ted replied. "*Mucho gusto.*"

Beside the native pastor stood a tall, muscular, teen-aged boy with similar features as their host. The girl's thought the combination of the tropical suit and hat that Pastor Jiménez wore was really cool and very GQ. Several of them, Wendy included, also whispered about how cute the teenager was. This earned her a sharp look from Rick, which she casually ignored. When Rick looked back at the teen, he saw the boy eyeing several of the girls. He flashed a gleaming smile at Wendy which caused of the girls to giggle and only served to make Rick even angrier.

The two ministers conversed like old friends while the group stood around taking in the sights and waiting for direction. After several minutes Ted reached over and shook hands with the tall boy. The trio turned together and approached the group.

"Alright, everyone," Ted said as the group gathered around him. When he had everybody's attention, he said, "This is Pastor Hector Jiménez and his son Juan."

Pastor Jiménez greeted them with a pleasant smile as he nodded to the group. "After you all retrieve your luggage, there is a bus waiting to take us to the church. I know you all are very tired from your flight, so we will make today's festivities short. There will be a small reception and meal, and then you will be divided up and introduced to your host families. They are all waiting to take you to your destinations, so let us get going and we will finish our introductions later."

After stowing their luggage in the bus, the group took their seats. Rick sat with Wendy in the third seat from the back. When the pastor's son, Juan, got on the bus, he took his time looking over everyone. As he panned the bus his eyes lingered once again on Wendy, infuriating Rick. The boy smiled and took the driver's seat. Pastor Jiménez and Ted sat directly behind him.

The ten-minute drive from the airport took them through downtown Mérida. Rick looked out the window, fascinated with the foreign city, but whenever he turned his attention back, he caught Juan glancing back through the rearview mirror at Wendy. He glared at the dark-haired teenager maliciously and resented the cocky attitude that the older teen seemed to emanate. He started wondering about the wisdom of crossing swords with the pastor's son, and for a brief moment he forgot all about the mission trip as he entertained the idea. Rick figured Juan was at least sixteen because he was driving the bus, unless the laws were more lax in Mexico than in the United States. That would make him two years older, putting Rick at a distinct disadvantage if they were to square off.

Wendy noticed Juan staring at her and blushed, bowing her head in what Rick thought was either embarrassment or flirtation. She leaned forward and whispered something to Mackenzie who was sitting in the seat in front of her. Rick couldn't hear what was said, but he couldn't help but notice Wendy and Mackenzie stifling giggles as they looked coyly at the driver. Rick wondered what Jim thought about the deliberate flirtation and if his friend was as offended as he was.

Arriving at the church, the group from the States were instructed to go inside the where their host families were gathered. Once they were seated, Pastor Jiménez addressed the group before him. Juan leaned against the door post and ogled at Wendy. Once again thoughts of putting the older teen in his place dominated Rick's thinking.

The two duelistas *stepped forward, standing three feet apart and staring fiercely at each other. The rugged and handsome* Americano *Rick Barber was fighting for the honor of the rich and incredibly beautiful* señorita *Wendy Patterson.*

Rick's opponent was the dastardly Juan Jiménez; the Scourge of the Yucatan. The roguish señor Jiménez had made daring advances toward the fair Wendy, and so a duel had been declared. Acting as Rick's second was best friend, the trusty Jim Farmer. He had brought a set of jewel-encrusted dueling paint guns which the two contestants were to shoot from twenty paces.

Rick stood boldly before the larger opponent, seeing in Juan's eyes the tiniest trace of fear. His enemy was having second thoughts. They stood back-to-back and waited for the count.

"One," Jim said.

Two steps were taken in opposite directions, one by each contestant. Rick took two deep breaths as he walked. Anyone watching him would probably remark that he had ice water in his veins.

Two...the weight of the pistola *felt heavy in his hand, but he knew he would be able to fire it when the time came.*

Three...Rick imagined Juan beginning to perspire, his nerves rubbed raw and placing him on edge.

Four...Rick felt a slight breeze and quickly calculated how much his shot would have to be adjusted to allow for the wind.

Five...Rick could almost see Juan's feet beginning to feel heavy and sluggish in the Mexican sand.

Six...Rick imagined his foe's breathing getting heavier.

Seven...only three more steps and history would be made.

Eight...Rick wondered if the coward would turn and fire early. There would be no honor in it, but Rick wouldn't put it past him.

Nine...one more step, and there would be paint spilled on Mexican soil.

"...ten young people that came with the Simons. We would like to start the introductions with Rick Barber and Jim Farmer."

Pastor Jiménez led the applause as the two club officers came forward. Rick was amazed that he was at the church, having no memory of ever leaving the bus or gathering his suitcase. All he could remember was thinking of ways to teach the pastor's son just who was boss.

Pastor Jiménez spoke a little more about the group and their accomplishments before introducing Rick and Jim to their host family.

"You will be staying with *Señor y Señora* Rogelio Galante," he said.

The *Galante* family consisted of Mr. and Mrs. *Galante* and their twelve-year-old son, Raúl. Mr. *Galante*, a medium tall man, had the same dark features as the rest of his countrymen. His wife possessed beautiful classic features with pouting lips and almond-shaped eyes. Their son had features similar to that of his father except for his eyes which were like his mother's.

Rick and Jim shook hands with the *Galante* family and followed them outside where they loaded their luggage into the back of an SUV. Rick was surprised at how well Raúl spoke English, until he learned that he had studied it in school since he was eight.

Rick caught a glimpse of Mackenzie and Wendy and the family they were staying with. Now that he was outside the church, he watched Juan help Wendy with her luggage. He wanted to go over and take over for him, but the *Galantes* were waiting to leave. As they pulled away from the church, Rick peered out the rear window for as long as he could until the church was out of sight.

As they drove westward toward the Galante's residence, Rick wondered at what point did he become so fixed on his animosity toward the pastor's son that he stopped noticing everything else around him. They had left the city limits of Mérida before he knew it. Raúl and Jim were talking about the four weeks ahead of them.

"Your group is all that Pastor Jiménez has talked about for weeks," Raúl said. "The church is very excited about all of you being here."

"We're excited to be here as well," Jim said. Looking at the passing countryside, Jim was taken in by its beauty. He had always thought of Mexico as mostly desert, with cacti and Joshua trees the only landscaping and clay *casas* or old mobile homes sprinkled about the desert scenery in a helter-skelter fashion.

"How far from Mérida do you live?" Jim asked.

Raúl seemed eager to answer Jim's questions about his home and country. Answering immediately, he said, "We live in Maxcanú, which is not all that far from Mérida."

"Rosa, that is my wife's name," Mr. Galante said, joining the conversation and appearing as eager to speak about his life with the visitors from the States as his son was, "wishes it was closer, but I like the freedom of being away from the traffic of Mérida. We have a five-hundred-acre ranch where we raise horses."

"Is that how you earn a living?" Rick asked, immediately regretting it as it sounded as if he was being nosey. "I'm sorry, that's none of my business," he apologized.

Mr. Galante reassured his guests. "Not at all; I own a shipping company, therefore it makes more sense to be located near the airport."

Rick nodded as if understanding the logistics of international trade and commerce. *After all*, he thought, *I just finished a report on business in Riverside, after interviewing Symcor, Trifax, and Consolitrak. Could a business in Mexico be much different?*

"Our ranch is only a small working ranch," *señor Galante* said modestly. "I have a *gaucho* named Alfonso who runs it and keeps everything in order."

The boys had no idea what it meant to be on a working ranch in Mexico, although Rick had an uncle in Montana who raised cattle. They pulled into a long access road that led to the "ranch house," which turned out to be quite large.

"I hope you do not mind, and we certainly did not do it out of disrespect, but we have set up living quarters for you in the bunkhouse," *señor Galante* said.

"That'll be fine," Rick replied, excited to stay in what he hoped would be a genuine Western experience.

"It is quite comfortable and should give you all the privacy you require. Also, while you are here, you will be able to select which horse will be yours. Raúl will teach you how to ride and take care of them."

At the mention of horses, both of the teens perked up and stared at each other, their eyes practically popping out of their heads with excitement. As they neared the *casa*, they saw behind it a full-sized swimming pool. Not exactly what they expected to find on a "working" ranch. In the corral beside the barn, there were about two dozen horses.

As they were unloading the car, señor *Galante* said, "After you get unpacked, Raúl will take you to the corral and you may select your horses."

Jim and Rick were led to the guest quarters by Raúl, which certainly wasn't what they expected a bunkhouse to be.

"My father had this converted and remodeled three years ago," Raúl said in the way of an explanation. "Since he is gone so much, we have downsized the ranch to only about fifty horses. We used to have over four hundred and were the largest ranch in the Yucatan."

The bunkhouse's décor was what came as a total surprise to the boys. Instead of roughly carved bunks with thin mattresses, there were several hammocks hung in strategic locations. The boys hung their clothes in tall wooden wardrobes and put their socks and underwear in the small chest of drawers that stood between the hammocks. The bunkhouse was still warm from the afternoon sun, but a slight breeze entered through the open windows and cooled them as they unpacked their bags.

Raúl showed them the shower that had been added with a sink and toilet at their disposal. "Towels and wash cloths can be found here," he said, opening a small linen closet. "You can put your laundry in this hamper and my mother will see that they are washed."

The boys thanked him and finished putting their things away. Afterwards, they rushed to the corral. Inside the fenced enclosure, an old *caballero* was feeding the horses. He had reddish, leathery skin with features that revealed a trace of Indian as well as his Mexican lineage and, in spite of being short and stocky, he had a long face and a sharp nose that was not typical among Mexicans. Though in his sixties, Rick was surprised at how well the man got around. He moved with the grace and coordination of someone with years of experience handling horses. The boys marveled at the way he went about performing his ranch duties, as the only hint to his age was his gray hair and wrinkles.

Raúl entered the corral with the boys and introduced them to Alfonso, who responded to the new arrivals warmly. "*Mucho gusto, se-ñor* Rick and Jim. Welcome to the Yucatan."

Rick shook hands with the old cowhand. "Thank you. We're glad to be here."

The boys walked slowly through the corral among the horses, hoping to find ones they liked but not knowing what to look for in a horse.

"Raúl, we're not really experienced riders," Rick confessed, looking sheepishly at his hosts.

"That is alright," Raúl said. "Alfonso and I can teach you. We just need for you to find a horse that you like."

After fifteen minutes or so, Jim had picked out a roan colored gelding and Rick a small mustang mare with brown and white spots. At first Rick selected a large piebald until Alfonso helped steer him away from it by telling him the horse was still a little wild.

After they finished selecting their horses, Raúl showed them the bridles and saddles, and showed them how to put each item on their horses.

"We do not usually name our stock horses, but you are free to choose a name for them if you wish," *señor* Galante said, entering the corral.

They had been concentrating so hard on learning how to put the bridles and saddles on their horses, they didn't even hear him approach. It took only a few seconds for the boys to think up names for their rides. Rick named his Ginger, not because he thought its color reminded him of the spice, but because he had seen plenty of reruns of *Gilligan's Island*, and thought it was just a "cool" name. Jim called his horse Starfire, because of its color and because of the star-shaped white marking on its face.

There was just enough time for a short ride before supper, so Raúl led the boys on a tour of the ranch. After their ride, Raúl demonstrated to his guests how to brush down the animals and put away the tack. Supper was served on the patio. After they ate, they waited the appropriate amount of time and then dove into the pool. The cool water was a pleasant relief from the humid temperature of the Yucatan afternoon. As they swam, *señor* Galante explained to them that tomorrow they would be taken back to the church to help work on the new sanctuary.

"It will be good to get it done. For some reason, the workers are not finishing the job fast enough. Your group came at just the right time. The entire project has been a pain in the neck."

That night, Rick and Jim lay in their hammocks discussing Juan, the pastor's son, and their impressions of him.

"The one thing that I noticed about him," Jim said, "was he really didn't mingle with the rest of the church people. In fact, he really didn't even greet *us*. I don't know if that means anything or not, but, if I get a chance, I'm going to ask Raúl about it."

They said goodnight to each other and soon dozed off as a steady breeze drifted through their window, carrying with it visions of open ranges, meals cooked over an open campfire, and cattle lowing on the prairie.

Chapter Four
Digging Foundations

On the third morning of their mission adventure, the three new friends were riding in the back of *señor* Galante's car on the way to the church. Taken back by the scenery and how it differed from his expectations of Mexico, a thought struck Rick. The day before, while meeting at the church, he noticed the main building looked very old but had been added on to several times.

"How long has the church been here," asked Rick?

Señor Galante slowed the car down as they entered a more congested traffic pattern, causing Rick to observe that rush hour traffic occurs even in Mexico.

"Our church was started about twenty years ago," Raúl's father said. "In fact, we were one of the families that helped start it, though Raúl wasn't born yet. Five years ago, our founding pastor died and pastor Jiménez has been here ever since."

"Was he the assistant before that?"

"Yes, and we were most blessed to have him. He was at one time an Olympic boxer. Pastor Gonzalez led him to the Lord shortly after the church began," *señor* Galante said. "Since then, the church has tripled in size. That is why we need the new sanctuary. Pastor Jiménez is a very popular minister in this region."

Rick thought about the information. Ever since the group started out to raise money for the building project, he had wondered about it.

"Are many of your members poor?" asked Rick. "I don't mean to be offensive, but you've seemed to outgrow your sanctuary, but your resources haven't seemed to keep up with the need."

If Mr. *Galante* seemed irritated at the remark, he didn't let it show.

"Sometimes, in your country, the same thing happens; no?"

Thinking about the answer, Rick quickly asked another question. "When was the current building erected? It looks really old."

Señor Galante laughed. "It is. It was built long before any of us were around. It began as an adobe mission by Franciscan monks back in 1617. Their work among the Mayans began right after Columbus discovered the new land. The land the church is on was given to the Franciscan order by a former Governor of the Yucatan. It wasn't government land though; it was one of his personal real estate holdings. Even though the church has been around for over four hundred years, nothing other than paving the parking lot and a few additions has been done to it. The paving took place seven years ago, and because we were outgrowing the church, we added onto the original structure also. Now we have to build again. We have already gone to multiple services, but that is taxing on the pastor and the musicians, plus you lose the feeling of closeness that is important for a church family. Of course, that happens with any large work, but we're hoping the new sanctuary will relieve that some. That's why we're excited to see what will happen when the new sanctuary is finished. It is designed to be flexible, and can be converted to an educational or administrative wing later on if the church continues to grow."

Arriving before anyone else, the boys said goodbye to Raúl's father and took time to examine for the first time at the task that lay before them. On the north side of the adobe mission the new construction had begun. Backhoes and bulldozers had moved earth and rock enough so that even a novice builder could discern a definite shape for the new structure. The other Gideon Ten members and the workers trickled in over the next twenty minutes.

"Where're Wendy and Mackenzie?" Rick asked as he noticed they hadn't arrived yet.

No one seemed to know, but as they thought about it, the church van arrived, driven by Juan. Wendy was in the front passenger seat.

Rick glared at the pastor's son, but Juan, when he noticed, only laughed to himself as he ignored Rick.

Thirty feet away, Jim whispered to Ken, "Do you think we have an international incident brewing?"

Ken smiled as he watched Rick's expression. "This could set relations between our country and Mexico back to the time just before the Alamo. What do you think Rick is going to do?"

Jim's expression darkened as he watched his best friend's suffering. "I'm not sure, but it wouldn't surprise me if someday the battle cry would be 'Remember the Yucatan.'"

Wendy did not appear to be ready for work as she was wearing shorts and a casual top. Her hair was pulled back in a ponytail. Even though her attire was more acclimated for a day at the beach, Rick noticed she even had a little makeup on her face. As she passed by the workers, the day laborers turned to watch her and Mackenzie. Several made comments in Spanish which Rick was thankful that he couldn't understand, though he deduced from the hand gestures and the leers the gist of the meanings.

Pastor *Jimenez* arrived and began dividing up the group. The girls were assigned the duty of gathering the loose stones and rocks that remained inside the foundation and the boys were issued shovels. The task of squaring up the sides with shovels seemed to Rick to be unnecessary, but there were still some larger rocks that had to be dislodged from the ground. Some of the boys were given the task of digging around the stones with their shovels. Then they would pick up the rocks and put them in wheelbarrows. Marcus and Terrell worked the wheelbarrows and emptied them, freeing the foundation of the debris.

Even though it was still before noon, the temperature had already reached ninety degrees. Rick noticed the heat didn't seem to bother Juan, Raúl, or the other workers as much as it did the boys from Riverside who were not accustomed to the intense humidity. They had already sweated through their shirts.

It was not exactly how Rick and Jim had envisioned the Lord's work, but he noticed that even Ted and Pastor Jiménez were working with picks and shovels, as well as five men from the construction company. It amused Rick to watch Ted struggle with the humidity also.

For the most part, the other men were helpful, instructing the boys on how to let their shovels do the work for them. One of the workers, a large Mexican who seemed to tower above the rest of his countrymen, not only resented the visitors but went out of his way to embarrass them by going over the areas they had finished and making a show of digging up what they had left behind. He was loud and his exaggerated movements made his dislike for the visitors obvious.

Pastor Jiménez watched one exchange between the large worker and Terrell, immediately correcting the man. The worker called himself *León*, which in Spanish meant lion and was probably only a nickname, even though no one seemed to know his real name. A day laborer who was paid at the end of each shift, he was broad with a rough face and a thick mustache. The pastor got upset when he heard the man refer to Terrell and Marcus as *chicitos negros*. The minister cornered the man, speaking to him harshly and rapidly in Spanish, his hands gesturing roughly what would have been the same as if spoken in English. Though the other man was larger than the pastor, it soon became apparent to anyone paying attention that the laborer feared the preacher. Pastor Jiménez continued berating the man as he waved his arms about in an aggressive manner.

Another man, Rocky, an American graduate student working in the Yucatan while he completed his thesis, rushed over to where the pastor and León stood arguing. Rocky had light reddish hair, and a long deeply-tanned face. Though smaller than León, he appeared to be the group's leader, keeping a close eye on the other four at all times.

"What's the problem here?" he asked.

Pastor Jiménez told the American about the taunting, taking the opportunity to give another warning glance at León.

"I am terribly sorry about this, Pastor Jiménez," Rocky said. He too shot León a nasty look. "I assure you it won't happen again."

When the minister walked away, Rocky stood in the corner with León, and the two men communicated in heated whispers. Rocky was clearly agitated, speaking angrily with his hands flying outward from his body in a frantic manner. He poked his finger into the larger man's chest as both looked toward the visitors.

When work resumed, Rick and the others seemed to feel the heat even more than before, though now they noticed that even the other workers were beginning to show the strain from the humidity.

Juan stripped off his shirt. His chest was firm and his washboard like stomach testified to the hours he had spent in a weight room. Rick was ashamed at the difference between the pastor's son and himself. Juan's biceps and forearms were well defined, and even though Rick knew he shouldn't compare himself with someone two years older, he couldn't help himself. He also noticed Wendy and the other girls glimpsing at Juan and blushing. As Pastor Jiménez watched his son's effect on the girls, his face took on an angry expression. In spite of his obvious displeasure, he said nothing to his son.

By three o'clock the temperature became too hot for the work to continue, as the sun bore down on them. It was siesta time. The crew had finished with the north part of the sanctuary so Pastor Jiménez called it quits for the day. As the workers ambled away, Rick glowered once again at Juan who strutted past him to pick up his shirt. Instead of putting it back on, he threw it over his shoulder in a cavalier manner as he escorted Wendy and Mackenzie back to the church van. The two girls continued to blush as he opened the door for them. Rick wasn't concerned about Mackenzie, and didn't know if Jim noticed or even cared, but he was nursing a slow boil as he watched the trio drive away.

Rick, Jim, and Raúl were the last to leave, but because they had to wait for Raúl's father to pick them up, the boys decided to work a little longer. Most of the day laborers had collected their money from Pastor Jiménez and left, turning their tools in at the south end of the excavation site. After twenty minutes of additional work, the trio decided to call it quits for the day as well. As they moved toward the place where the tools were stored, something caught Rick's eye. He didn't know if it was a glint from the sun or not, but he walked over to it and tried to nudge the shiny object with his toe. It held fast. He poked around it with his shovel and it made a small clanking sound.

The item appeared to be a piece of golden metal barely sticking out of the soil. Rick pried it with the edge of his shovel, after removing the dirt from around it, and, with the help of Jim and Raúl, he was able to dig out a small wooden chest about the size of a shoebox. It was made from a dark, mahogany-like wood and the corners were reinforced by metal. Rick's adrenaline began pumping as he realized the metal was gold plated. *The box must have been very expensive at one time, but what was it doing buried in the ground?* Rick wondered.

The boys tried opening the small chest, but it was held shut by an intricate latch that had a keyhole in the middle of it. Jim turned his head and noticed León and Rocky standing at the southern edge of the dig site. Jim nudged Rick as soon as he saw the two men, but they seemed to have come out of nowhere. Rick thought everyone had left for the day. It made him nervous the way the two men kept staring at them and whispering. Their actions hinted to more than just a casual interest in what the boys were doing.

"We're being watched," Jim whispered, "but don't look up. Be casual."

"I know," Rick answered with a hint of fear in his voice. "I've been watching them watching us. Let's get out of here, but not in a hurry, just nice and easy."

León had just climbed back into the hole. His mouth was turned upward in a cruel snarl as approached the three boys. At the same time, a car horn sounded behind him. The day worker turned to see *señor* Galante waving and urging the boys to come quickly.

Rick picked up the box and his shovel, and the three boys hurried past León. Putting their tools with the rest, the boys raced to the car. As they drove away, Rick looked back and saw León and Rocky watching them and talking. He continued to watch them until they were out of sight. Rick wondered if they knew what the box was or if they were just naturally curious. He held the box up and studied it again. *What was in it and what was it doing buried in the ground? How long had it been there?* Rick thought again about León and Rocky. He got the impression that they knew something about it. He wondered if they had some idea about what was in it. Was that the reason they were working on this particular project? Either way it didn't matter, because Rick knew without a doubt that Juan was not the only enemy he would make on this trip.

The boys waited until after supper before investigating the old box, though the delay made Rick feel like a five-year old longing for Christmas. Supper seemed to drag along mercilessly, but the boys rushed through it, causing *señora* Galante to comment on the way they finished the meal so fast.

"Is there a custom in the states for teenagers to eat as quickly as possible?" she asked.

Señor Galante shrugged his shoulders in response as he watched the boys leave.

Rick and Jim said nothing as they followed Raúl out the door. Instead of going for a ride, which would have taken too much time to cool down the horses afterwards and put the tack away, the boys swam a little to cool down before retiring to the bunkhouse. Raúl had moved some of his things into the bunkhouse with Rick and Jim, deciding it would be fun to have roommates, even if it was for only a few weeks. Before they brought the chest out from behind its hiding place, Raúl went to the door, cracked it open, and peeked outside.

"Okay, I do not see Alfonso anywhere," he said. He went to the large wardrobe where Rick had stored his clothes and took the chest from the bottom. Rick and Jim gathered beside Raúl as he unwrapped the box. At first they couldn't even budge the clasp that held the lid shut, but eventually Raúl was able to insert the tip of his pocket knife blade into the keyhole. He twisted the handle and heard a satisfying click as the mechanism fell away. At first he thought he had picked the lock perfectly, mentioning it to the other two, but then he realized that is was only because the lock had been corroded. "Instead of me picking it, it just fell away," he explained.

The lid rose stiffly on the rusted hinges, but Raúl inserted the knife's blade into the gap and pried the chest open. Peering inside the small box, they saw a knife, several small coins, and a book wrapped in lambskin. The hasp of the knife was encrusted with jewels and engraved in Spanish with the name *capitán Enrique de la Casa de Sangre*. The gold coins had the image of a woman on them. Raúl had to admit that he had never seen any coins like them before. The book turned out to be in Spanish as well. The first page read *el cuaderno de bitácora del tiberón del océano*. At the bottom was the signature of *capitán Enrique de la Casa de Sangre*.

"What does it mean," Rick asked.

Raúl's eyes grew as large as quarters and his voice cracked as he answered. "It says that it is the ship log of the Ocean Shark. It is written in Spanish and signed by Captain Enrique Sangre. Actually, his full last name means 'of the House of Blood.'"

Chapter Five

Captain Enrique
de la Casa de Sangre's Log

"Captain Blood? Isn't that the name of an old movie, or something?" Jim asked as he picked up the dagger and reexamined it. Turning it over slowly, he paid careful attention to how the jewels sparkled in the dying sunlight. Along the edge of the rusted blade was a dark reddish stain that he recognized as dried, caked on blood.

"That is what his name means," Raúl said. "The book appears to be very old, just like the knife. In fact, the first date is from September of 1603."

"So, what's it doing buried in the dirt in the middle of the Yucatan?" Rick asked.

Raúl shrugged his shoulders and shook his head. "I do not know, but I think it might be made clear if we read the log."

"What time is it now, Rick?" Jim said.

Rick looked at his watch. "It's almost nine o'clock. Maybe we can read it until…say midnight?"

"Won't that be a little late?" Jim said. "We still have to go to work tomorrow."

Rick responded with a mischievous smile. "Let's try for eleven, and then decide. It might just be an interesting story."

Agreeing to the time limit, Raúl carefully began turning the pages of the logbook, feeling as if he was voyaging through time, as he read and interpreted the words.

16-9-1603 received commission while at cartagna. took on three additional mates.

19-9-1603 set sail for havanna. chance to trade spices for tobacco and gunpowder. settin sail with ten crewmen short. will have to take on additional mates once we have landed.

22-9-1603 made excellent time. fair winds holdin tho dark clouds be a gatherin westward. will pull in and wait out latest storm.

25-9-1603 signed on seven more crewmen. three others have deserted the ship. have shipment for port at caracas. will leave by 1 october. crew not be likin the island hoppin. want to be makin a more prosperous living. possible mutiny but will not let them take me ship.

1-10-1603 underway to caracas. full crew on board. trade winds are blowin kindly. should make in less than two days.

3-10-1603 made port in caracas.

"Is that all he talks about?" Rick asked as he paced back and forth. He found the language of the old log boring. "That's just a bunch of hiring and firing and moving bananas around."

Raúl turned several pages at once, skimming over the words as he thumbed to the next entrée. "Let me skip a few months and see if there is anything more exciting," Raúl said. "What time is it?"

Rick looked at his watch and answered, "It's ten forty-five."

Raúl gave an impish grin. "Okay, let me skip to 1604 and see if they moved any mangoes along with all of those bananas."

3-1-1604 crewmen are getting restless for adventure. several have talked about upping profits by smugglin or even piratin. keepin me eye on first mate panchez. insurrection could be in the near future.

5-1-1604 heard tell of a spanish fleet called the terra firma flota. first mate told of scheduled move from cartagena to havanna by way of the yucatan peninsula. seven ships to move gold and spices. will keep an ear open for more information.

7-1-1604 ship loaded and crew ready to depart. ocean shark departure delayed by late season hurricane. will be unable to set sail from kingston harbor safely.

9-1-1604 two ships arrived in kingston. both in bad shape. caught in hurricane. five other ships unaccounted for. believed to be thrown agin the serranilla banks and lost. citizens organizin rescue mission. will leave day after tomorrow.

10-1-1604 slipped out of harbor at early light. winds still heavy but we are usin the shelter of darkness and high winds to keep rescuers away from us. should make serranilla banks by noon tomorrow.

11-1-1604 found two ships crippled but still afloat. faced little resistance while boarding. transferred cargo of gold ore and spices. took on ten new crewmen. scuttled the ships. Cargo contained enough gold and spices to be amountin to a small fortune. left area before being spotted by rescue ships from kingston.

Raúl's father knocked on the door and said, "Boys? Seven o'clock comes really early, especially if you don't get any sleep."

Jim and Rick looked at Raúl, their stares containing an element of fear.

"It is alright; he is not mad. Just giving us a subtle hint," Raúl said as he placed the logbook back in the wooden chest. "We will have to finish this tomorrow evening." He reached over to turn off the lamp.

"Wait," Rick said as he jumped out of his hammock. "I don't know why, but I think we need to find a better place hide the box. I'd feel better about it."

Jim and Raúl agreed. "Do you want to put it back in the wardrobe?" Jim asked.

Rick appeared to think it over as he started toward the wardrobe.

Before he could stow the chest away, Raúl jumped up and said, "Wait a minute. Let me have that knife." Taking the ancient weapon from Jim, he placed it inside the chest along with the log book. Crossing the room, he cracked open the door leading to the stables and checked outside. Then he took a chair from beside the desk, climbed up, and placed the chest on a shelf beside the door and gently pushed it until it disappeared.

"There is a small drop-off behind this shelf. I found it a couple of years ago. We will have to use a chair to get it out tomorrow, but at least nobody will find the chest."

The three boys drifted off to sleep, each with their own ideas of how to use the information they had gathered. Raúl was curious about the outcome of the ship known as the *tiberone*, Jim about how the blood had come to be caked along the edge of the knife, and Rick about the captain turned pirate who called himself *Enrique de la Casa de Sangre*.

The open sea has always been the perfect place for a man of adventure; the spray of salty water with taut sails billowing, straining against the gust of strong trade winds. Captain Rick de la Barber de la Riverside stood on the bridge, one hand steady on the helm, the other wrapped around the hilt of his cutlass. His first mate, Juan, the cowardice scourge of the Yucatan, needed to be watched. He had been seen skulking in the dark corners, holding secret communications with some of the crew members. The fleeting glances. The unheard whispers.

Captain Rick knew the true reason for the mutiny was not the booty, it was the fair maiden, señorita Wendy de la casa de la Patterson de la Riverside, a ravenous redhead of rapturous beauty. They had met during the last raid of Jamaica. Along with the treasures and spices taken in the raid, Captain Rick had made her acquaintance while dining at the Jolly Roger, a lowly diner that served the best pizza in the Caribbean. Unfortunately, the fearful Juan saw them, and instantly, enamored with the maiden's beauty, became hopelessly jealous. He had been plotting the overthrow of Captain Rick ever since.

They had just passed over the Serranilla Banks, when someone threw a dagger at Captain Rick, the murderous missile barely missed him and imbedded itself in the mast beside his head. The experienced seaman knew immediately what had to be done. He would steer the vessel to Mérida and turn the entire crew of pirates over to the authorities, where they would be denied chocolate and Nintendo for at least five years.

The attack came quickly from starboard side as three crewmen grabbed hold of Captain Rick and shook him. Captain Rick held tough, determined to see justice done. He fought off the cowards as he held firmly to the wheel. His attackers were relentless, screaming at him, calling his name...

"Rick, you've got to get up now."

Rick opened his sleep-filled eyes to mere slits, expecting to see Juan and two coconspirators. Instead he found Raúl, Jim and *señor* Galante standing over him.

"Are you awake yet?" Jim said.

"Yeah, I'm fine," Rick mumbled like a drunken sailor. "I guess I didn't sleep so good last night." He got up, stumbled to the sink and splashed water on his face. The cold liquid ran down his neck and inside his T-shirt before he could grab a towel.

"Señor Rick, please get dressed. We need to leave in fifteen minutes," *señor* Galante said as he closed the door to the bunkhouse.

The boys got dressed in ten minutes, and thirty minutes later they were dropped off at the church for breakfast and another day's work.

Even so, the boys' minds were fixed on a wooden box hidden behind a shelf in the bunkhouse. It would be at least eight hours before they could read through it again. The wait would make the day seem even longer.

Chapter Six

An Unexpected Visitor

The second day of work was even harder than the first; the sun hotter, the rocks heavier, and the dirt dirtier, but Jim, Rick, and Raúl somehow found a way to survive, mainly because their minds were fixed on the little chest hidden behind a shelf in the bunkhouse. Rick didn't even pay attention to Wendy and Juan as they sat by themselves while eating their lunch, He didn't take time to worry about Rocky, who seemed to go out of his way to work closely beside them. He didn't even give León's absence a second thought. The stocky day laborer failed to show up for work that morning, but no one seemed to really miss his company. As soon as *señor* Galante arrived to pick up the boys, they ran to the car and jumped in, anxious to get home.

"You boys must be in a hurry," he said as he steered the car into traffic. "How did it go today?"

"Just fine, Dad," Raúl said as he turned his attention to his new friends. The boys made small talk on the ride home, being careful not to speak of the box they had discovered the day before. After arriving home, they even refused the invitation to go swimming from Raúl's mother, stating they were going to wait until after supper.

Opening the door to the bunkhouse, they stopped at the threshold in a state of shock. Their suitcases were on the floor and the contents of the wardrobes strewn about the room. Boxes and furniture were upended and Jim's hammock was torn down. The curtains framing one of the windows hung at a peculiar angle with the rod almost ripped away from the wall. The window was cracked open wider than when they left. The boys instantly thought the same thing as they ran toward the shelf. Placing a chair in front of it, Raúl climbed up and reached carefully into the gap, bringing out the wooden chest.

"Well, at least whoever did this didn't find it. Should we tell your father about this?" Jim asked.

Raúl's face grew taut as he contemplated and answer. "I don't know. If we tell him about the break-in, we'll have to tell him about the chest also. Do you want to do that?" Raúl said.

Rick set the chest on the desk, picked up his suitcase, and crammed his clothes into it. He said, "No. Right now, we need to clean this place up," he said loudly as he threw the case onto the bottom of the wardrobe. "After that we're going to find out what happened to Captain King of the Zombies, and then we're going to make citizen's arrests, receive our rewards, and get on the plane back to Riverside."

Raúl and Jim were taken back by Rick's outburst. Jim had always known Rick to be a little impetuous at times, but he had never seen him that emotionally upset, not even when he missed the fly ball that lost his team's baseball game against University City.

"Rick, what's the problem?" Jim asked. "I've never seen you like this."

"Problem? There's no problem," he hollered as he continued throwing his clothes back inside the suitcase as if he had only five minutes to catch his flight out of Mexico. "I mean, how many times in a person's life does their stuff get picked through by some stranger, and how many more enemies are we going to make on this trip?"

Jim knew exactly how Rick felt. They had been violated, just as if someone had read their mail or learned all of their most intimate secrets, but what he couldn't understand was how quickly Rick went to pieces over the matter.

"Look, Rick, I feel the same way you do," said Jim, "but you can't fall apart at something like this, especially after how you led us through the burglary investigation in Riverside. You're stronger than that. And what's this about making enemies? I don't understand what's going on inside your head? I've noticed you watching Juan and Wendy, but if you want my opinion, there's nothing going there, so what enemies have you made? Nobody's threatened you that I know of. Even León only seemed threatening, but we don't know that he's an enemy for sure yet."

Raúl suppressed a smile as he said, "I know I'm not as old as you, but maybe you should count the number of friends you've made since you've been here instead of the number of enemies."

Rick wanted to block out the words, preferring instead to stew in his own anger and self-pity, but instead he stopped, hung his head slightly, and took a deep breath, allowing it to seep out slowly. His face turned a bit red as he apologized for his abrupt reaction.

"Rick, it's not wrong to complain," Jim said. "We all do it sometime sooner or later. The main thing is to get over it. Come on."

Rick nodded. "You're right. Come to think of it, everybody needs a voice of logic and conscience every once in a while, but even Pinocchio had only *one* Jiminy Cricket. What did I ever do to deserve two?"

The boys laughed, slapping Rick on the back Even Rick joined in as the tension drifted like a puff of smoke from the room. The cleanup of the bunk house didn't take very long. They had almost finished straightening up the room when Jim thought of something else.

"Why don't we go outside and check for clues!"

The boys stopped cleaning and checked the corral as they rounded the building to see if Alfonso was around. They found him working with one of the horses, but made sure he didn't see them as they weren't prepared to answer any questions and hoped he wouldn't ask. Arriving at the rear of the bunkhouse they approached the window where the curtain had been torn down.

On the soft earth beneath the window sill they found several footprints. Kneeling beside them, Jim said, "Wish I knew how to make a plaster cast, not that it would help us."

"Right! The only two people we know who would care about a plaster cast," Rick explained to Raúl, "would be Ken or Kim, and they would probably question the technique in which we gathered it more than the cast itself."

"That's right," Jim conceded, "besides, we can't prove that the footprint belongs to the same person who broke into our room."

Raúl knelt by the footprints and began probing the edges with his finger. "No, but we can safely *assume* that they do. This print doesn't belong to anyone from around here."

"How do you know?" asked Rick kneeling beside him.

"These were not made by cowboy boots," Raúl said, pointing at the rounded toes of the prints. "Cowboy boots are pointed at the toes and they're the only shoes that Alfonso wears. They also don't belong to my father, because he mostly wears dress shoes. Besides, his feet are much smaller and so are ours. We mostly wear tennis shoes."

Raúl stuck his index finger along the edge of one print. "These prints were made by heavy work boots and from a pretty big man. You can tell not only by the size of them, but also from how deep they are sunk in the dirt? A heavy man made these."

"Does Alfonso or your father smoke?" Rick asked, pointing to a cigarette butt a few feet from the print.

"No," Raúl answered, "but that's the same brand that someone at the job site smokes."

"You mean someone like León, who wasn't at work today?" Jim asked. A conspiratorial look passed along the three boys.

"I'd say so," Rick agreed, nodding his head as he stared at the prints.

"If it *was* León, you can bet that Rocky sent him. And you can also guess what they were after. Let's get back inside and finish cleaning up," Rick said. "Then we can examine that log some more and see what all the fuss is about."

They had just finished resetting the bunkhouse when *señora Galante* called them for supper. After eating they rode for an hour before returning to the bunkhouse. Raúl opened the chest, being careful not to force it too hard, and pulled out the log. Turning to the page where he had left off the previous night, he began reading.

12-1-1604 have sailed beyond the serranilla banks. moving northwest toward the yucatan channel. ship damaged by high winds and over laden with cargo taken from pero océano and tigre aqua. after we pass through the yucatan channel we best be finding a port.

16-1-1604 first mate sanchez has been avoiding me. we have passed beyond the yucatan channel. accordin to the sexton and the position of the stars, we are at the western edge of the yucatan peninsula. we will have to find a quiet cove to be pullin into.

18-1-1604 have anchored ship inside a small, overgrown bay. we were able to lower the sails and usin the oars we hid it from any traffic from the gulf. have kept unwanted land lubbers away by postin guards who scare any intruders away with odd noises and strange lights. noises from the guards usin reeds and wood whistles and lights created by coverin the lanterns with red silk.

23-1-1604 ship may be more damaged than at first feared. main mast is cracked and the hull is eaten up with dry rot. have visited mérida on several occasions. no place for repairs. town is agricultural center. rumors be reportin our cove is haunted. the local natives have begun calling it superstition cove. i fear that superstition will not keep our identity secret for long.

31-1-1604 two weeks since we made land. crew is getting restless. first mate sanchez is the worst of the bunch. he has not been openly challenging of me yet but the time be approachin near.

5-2-1604 returned from town late. was attacked by two mates. was able to kill them both. sanchez is behind the attack. will have to dispose of him.

6-2-1604 caught Sanchez by the waterside. slit his throat and dragged his body into the jungle. gutted the body to draw the jaguars. crew is now scared. believing their own superstitions. sixteen men have deserted the last three days. have decided to scuttle the ship and move the treasure to a different spot.

10-2-1604 have used grottos to drop bodies in. am the only survivor now. will move to mérida. have enough bounty to join society. the ship is at the bottom of the cove. time to be movin' on.

5-7-1604 have purchased much land. treasure has been hidden. moved half of it to a spot off the edge of the jungle. will get it when needed. have lowered the rest into a grotto. area has six of them. can get it when be needin it. no one alive to be recognizin me. am now a gentleman of means.

12-12-1606 have been accepted into society. my new wealth has earned me the title of mayor of mérida. will get the remainder of gold someday. located in the cenote at the northeasternmost edge of the jungle.

Juan closed the log, carefully placing it back in the chest. Silence hovered over them like a death shroud, suffocating the boys with what they had read. This wasn't a pirate movie on television whose intention was to entertain. This was real life. This was the confession of a mass murderer. The manifested evil they had just read about shocked them to their bones. First, he had killed innocent sailors instead of offering to rescue them. After he killed them, he stole their goods and gold. Then he killed his own crew one by one, the very men who had sailed with him. In the end they meant nothing to him. The man had lived up to his name after all. Blood.

"There's just one thing that I don't understand," Rick said, breaking the silence. "What are these grottos that the log talks about?"

Raúl, walked to his hammock and climbed in, turning on his side to face him.

"We have no above ground rivers here in the Yucatan," he began in the way of explanation, "but the grottos are like underground caverns, and they run throughout the entire peninsula. The salt water flows in, gets filtered by the limestone and becomes purified enough to sustain life and crops."

"I was just wondering," Rick said, "could you be able to show us one?"

"S...s...sure, we can go sometime."

Rick felt Raúl's hesitancy. "Look, Raúl, I know this is asking a lot, but we're only going to be here another two weeks. Tomorrow's Saturday, and I know we can sleep in, but I was wondering, can you find the area where these grottos are?"

Raúl smiled brightly and his dark eyes glistened. He had heard some of the other members tell stories about Rick's passion for adventure. Now he knew it was true. "You want to try and find the treasure, don't you?"

Rick knew it wasn't an accusation, but just a remark to clarify his intentions. He nodded. "It had crossed my mind."

"I know of some bays that fit the description," Raúl said. "They're about five miles from here. We can take the horses out for a ride and just look around."

They all agreed. Instead of sleeping in, they would get up early, saddle the horses, and take a ride to the area that Raúl thought was once called Superstition Cove. That night they all three slept, but their dreams were mostly of the same things; gold, silver, and danger.

Chapter Seven

The Lost Pirate Cove

The next morning the three boys were up even before Alfonso or Raúl's parents. They saddled their horses for the short ride to the coast and led them away from the bunkhouse before mounting in order to not alert Alphonso of their departure. The very action reminded Rick and Jim of the night Ken and Marcus sneaked out to scout the mall.

Ginger responded easily to Rick's guidance. Both boys from the states appeared to be more experienced riders than they really were as Starfire was also gentler than even Jim thought. Raúl rode a tawny-colored quarter horse named Samson.

The morning was almost perfect, with a cool breeze blowing in from the west. The clouds above their heads were full and fluffy and as they rode the three *amigos* looked for shapes. Rick could only see pirate ships for some reason, so he allowed the other two to use their imagination without interruption. They arrived at the Gulf side coast around 9:30. Raúl led them through the tropical forests, cautioning them to keep a watch out for any wild cats. He warned them that it would be rare to face one during the daytime hours, but it was still prudent to be on the lookout, because they could strike with such speed that you would never have time to react.

The underbrush was thick. Even though much of the coast had become commercialized, there were still pockets that hadn't been developed. Rick was glad he wore his blue jeans instead of the shorts he first thought of putting on.

They had been following the coast for about twenty minutes when Raúl reigned in his horse. He dismounted, tied Samson to a limb, and waited for the other two to follow his example. After Rick and Jim had dismounted and secured their horses, Raúl forced his way through some foliage until they came to a spot about forty feet off the trail. He made his way to a hole in the ground that was about five feet in diameter. He called the others over to look at it but warned them to be cautious.

"What is it?" Rick asked.

Raúl picked up a small pebble and dropped it down the hole. Three seconds later the boys heard a feint splash. "Did you hear that? This is a small grotto," he said.

"How deep is it?" Rick asked.

"It's hard to say," Raúl said. "The water levels change as the grottos erode."

Jim stood and looked around. "Is this where he hid the treasure?"

Raúl shook his head. "This is not the right bay. There are only two grottos in this area. The bay described by the logs had six of these. I think I know which one it is. It's closer to Sisal. It's not overgrown anymore, but it hasn't been fully developed yet either."

"How far is it?" Jim asked.

"Only a few miles. Maybe we can…" He stopped talking and started listening intently to the jungle. The horses were whinnying and pawing the ground, reacting to something.

Raúl looked about cautiously. His eyes were alert and reflected the fear he was sensing. "We'd better be moving on," he said. "The horses sense something. I don't want to meet a big cat out here unprotected."

"What kind of big cat?" Rick asked. In his mind he was thinking of jaguars or cougars.

Rushing through the overgrowth, Raúl mounted Samson and waited for the other two to climb on their horses. As if reading Rick's mind, Raúl said, "Probably not a jaguar this far north, but it could be an ocelot. Something has them spooked. It would be best if we didn't stay and find out."

Raúl led them further up the coast, but as they rode the wind began picking up, the gentle breeze became stronger. Within minutes, the temperature had dropped and the sky to the east appeared as black as midnight with intermittent lighting flashes.

"Is that a storm coming in?" Rick asked.

Raúl shook his head. "It might rain a little. I heard my father say something about Hurricane Beverly yesterday. We're just now beginning the hurricane season and this is only the second storm. It's supposed to miss us and move north toward Cuba and Florida. Of course, no one can really predict these things."

"Are we in any danger?" Jim said, cautiously watching the darkening clouds.

"We should be alright. We'll be home before anything happens."

Jim and Rick followed Raúl toward Sisal, keeping a close eye on the eastern horizon with a mounting sense of trepidation. Raúl finally stopped them near a private cove. The area was large with a small outlet opening outward to the Gulf.

"Four hundred years ago," Raúl explained, pointing at the cove, "this entire area would have been overgrown. The bay's opening would have been almost totally hidden. With the jungle coming out almost to the beach, it would have been the ideal place to anchor a ship. They would have been hidden from casual observers and the guards would frighten away the rest."

"That means at the bottom of this cove we'll find the ruins of the Ocean Shark," Rick said excitedly.

"Maybe," Raúl said with a note of caution. "But there are other coves like this one. I just thought of this one because I know of six grottos in this area. Let me show you."

Raúl led them to the southern edge of the cove, stopping about twenty feet from the jungle's perimeter. Pointing at the ground, he showed them the first hole. Then he signaled for them to follow him. He led them to five more grottos over a stretch of a quarter of a mile.

Two of the grottos were large enough to drop cars into. At the sixth hole, the boys tied their horses to a nearby tree.

"Didn't the log say that the treasure was in the grotto at the northeast part of the cove?" Rick asked trying to recall what they had read the night before.

"It did, but the jungle isn't the same as when *Enrique de la casa de Sangre* wrote his diary." Raúl walked back to the fourth hole. "The closest one to the northeast would be this one. It's large, but I don't think that it's the right one."

Jim and Rick edged closer to the grotto. Raúl leaned over it and peered into the inky blackness. Then he returned to his horse, opened the backpack that was draped over its saddle horn, and retrieved his flashlight. Switching it on, he directed the ray down into the coal black pit. The beam created by the halogen lamp split the darkness of the underground cave, only to be swallowed by the completeness of its void. Raúl dropped a large stone into the hole. The resounding splash was now heard about two seconds later.

"Is that deep?" asked Jim.

"We could ask Ken or Kim," Rick answered, "but I think it's about a forty-foot drop. Do we have any rope, Raúl?"

Raúl shook his head. "Not enough that would make it safe to lower you down there. Besides, it's not getting you in there that's the hard part. It's getting you out. At that distance, it would take two of us to lift one person. That would mean whoever went in would have to go in alone. I know I don't want to volunteer."

"Couldn't we use the horses to pull us up?" Rick said.

Raúl thought about it before answering. "It's possible, but it would also be risky. We don't know what is down there exactly. First of all, we're only guessing about the depth, and then there could be some strong currents as well. It would be very dangerous."

Not to be deterred, Rick contemplated the currents, but wondered how bad they could be. "What about diving in the cove and searching for the ship?" Rick said.

"We don't have any scuba gear," Raúl explained. "Besides, the riptide could just as easily carry you out to sea. Unless you're a really strong swimmer, you'd be two miles out into the gulf before your body would surface. We're going to have to find another way to look into this."

The soft rumble of thunder in the background reminded them of the approaching storm. Turning toward the east, they saw the sky had become even darker and the wind more fierce than before. Having given all of their attention to the grottos, the boys had forgotten about the potential downturn in the weather.

"What were you saying about that hurricane?" Rick said as they raced for the horses.

The wind roared like a runaway freight train as it forced its way through the trees, snapping leaves and whipping branches as it came. One branch crashed to the ground fifteen feet away, frightening the horses. They pulled at the reins in an attempt to free themselves from the limbs they were tethered to. The boys were able to grab the reins of their horses just in time. Jumping onto the saddles, they turned the horses into the wind. As their horses picked up speed and started for home, the rain began falling. With over ten miles to ride, the three teens knew they would be soaked to the bone by the time they arrived, but they didn't want to be caught out in the open if the storm worsened.

Lightning flashed and thunder crashed, as the horses sped into the slashing downpour. The storm fell in heavy sheets across their trail, blinding them, but they continued to push bravely into the storm. The rain felt like needles piercing their skins as it pelted them. The sand beneath the horses flying hooves became muddy, slowing their progress.

Once they reached the ranch, the boys led their mounts into the barn. Although their clothes were thoroughly soaked and they were cold, they took the time to rub their horses down first and put oats in their feeders. After putting away the tack, they ran to the bunkhouse where they changed into dry clothes before donning jackets and rushing to the house.

Crashing through the kitchen door, they were met by *señora* Galante who was taking freshly baked *chimichangas* from the oven.

"I wondered when you boys were going to come in to eat. Have you been sleeping all this time?"

"Not exactly," Raúl said, but he withheld any further information. "What's happening with this storm? I thought it was supposed to miss us?"

"The television weatherman said that it turned last night, drifting southward, and has gained strength. They believe the storm should pass through the Yucatan during the next forty-eight hours. Word has already gone out about cancelling church services for tomorrow. Also there will be no work on the building on Monday until they can assess the storm's damage. Then Pastor Jiménez will bring in some workers to clean up the mess created by the storm. So you boys can sleep in for the next two days as well."

Finishing their meal, they dodged puddles and raindrops as they ran back to the bunkhouse. After drying off, they retrieved the book from its hiding spot. Raúl had just started reading from it when he heard a soft knock at the door. When he opened the door, he found Alfonso standing outside.

"Hi, Alfonso. Did you need something?"

"No, señor Raúl," the old cowhand said as he stuck his head into the room. "I want to tell our guests how pleased I am that they are taking such wonderful care of their horses. I appreciate you taking the time to brush them down and put fresh oats in their bags, and also for putting the tack away. I'd better get back out there. The storm has the horses jumpy. I just wanted to say thanks."

The boys thanked him for his compliment and asked if he needed any help with the horses, but he declined. After he left, Rick asked,

"Do you think he suspects anything?"

Raúl thought about it. "I think he knows we were out, but that's probably all."

"Will he tell your parents?"

Raúl shook his head as he reopened the logbook. "Not unless he's asked."

The boys read the pages that were recorded between February 10th and December 12th two years later, coming to the conclusion that there wasn't enough information to determine if they had found the right cove or not.

"We need some help," Rick said. "We need to know how deep that grotto is, and Ken and Kim can tell us, unless you have a better idea."

"What would that do for us?" Jim asked.

"I don't know, but I'd like to know about the grottos in that area."

"Maybe we can find out about them on Monday," Raúl said. "There's a museum in Mérida that we can visit. It might hold some clues for us."

"How can looking at dinosaur bones help us?" Jim said.

"You'll see on Monday," Raúl said, giving his guests a cryptic grin. "You'll see."

Chapter Eight
The Historical Museum
of the Yucatan

Hurricane Beverly hit the Yucatan like an all-pro lineman going after an opposing quarterback. By the time it had crossed the peninsula it had uprooted trees, overturned cars and buses, and been downgraded to a tropical storm, not that any of the visitors from the states could tell the difference as it felt like a full-blown hurricane to them. Wendy and Mackenzie were upset because the cellular service was knocked out so they couldn't call home, and Marcus was petrified almost as much as the time when he was trapped in an empty grave in the cemetery while being chased by a gang of thieves. Still, everyone was thankful that none of the group from the states had been injured, even though the news reported that five people had been killed.

The boys were content with staying secure in the bunkhouse as the winds howled outside. Alfonso and *señor Galante* had boarded up the windows in preparation of the storm. The electricity stayed on, so they watched television and talked about pirate treasure for two days.

Since there was no work being done on the church, Raúl talked his father into taking them to the natural museum. *Señor Galante* reluctantly agreed, but only because he couldn't foresee any possible problem. That Monday the boys rode to Mérida with Raúl's father and were dropped off in front of *el Museo de Historía Naturál*. Because the museum didn't open for another hour and a half, Raúl said, "I know a place where we can have breakfast."

They walked two blocks to a small café where the boys ordered breakfast burritos. What was placed on the plates before them was not what the boys from the states were accustomed to. "These are hu-mongous!" Jim said, not believing the size of the burrito on his plate. "Certainly not what I expected."

Rick laughed, knowing Jim's only experience previously with breakfast burritos would have been at a fast food restaurant, and it probably took two to fill him.

Finishing their breakfast, the boys walked back to *el Museo de Historía Naturál*, arriving just as the doors were opening. "This place has more information about the Yucatan's intricate system of grottos than anybody," Raúl said, leading them inside. "As I told you, we have no rivers like you do in the states. Instead, all of our rivers are under-ground. They help to form the grottos that are also called cenotes," Raúl said. "They have displays here that show you how they are formed and how they are interconnected."

Rick wondered how learning about the water system would help them find the pirate's treasure, a subject that seemed to consume his every waking moment ever since Raúl read about it. Even so, he was fascinated with the displays, especially the ones that explained how the systems were formed and how they collapsed and reformed all over again. He studied the display that explained the process, looked at the photographs, and examined the models.

By noon they all felt hungry and decided to go out to eat. Rick and Jim were pleased to find a McDonalds in Mexico. Rick had heard about a pineapple burger that McDonalds served only in Hawaii. He wondered if they served anything crazy like an avocado burger or something equally as strange in Mexico, but he didn't see it on the large board behind the counter. He and Jim ordered their regular meal of Big Mac, fries, and a cola, which helped them fulfill their need to sustain their American culinary habits. While finishing the last of his fries, Raúl suggested they visit the *Biblioteca de Mérida*.

"What for?" said Rick.

"They keep all sorts of land records," Raúl replied. He took the last bite of his Big Mac and said, "I'd like to read about the mayor of Mérida in the early 1600's."

Jim looked up from his sandwich. "That's a great idea. I'd like to see what identity Captain Blood took after killing his men and stealing all the gold."

Ten minutes after leaving McDonalds, the boys arrived at the *Biblioteca de Mérida*. Raúl asked the librarian how to search for the information they needed. Going to the shelves, he pulled down a journal dated 1600 to 1625. The journal showed that the mayor between 1606 and 1610 was a nobleman and land owner named *Don Enrique Cortez*. *Don Cortez* went on to become the Governor of the Yucatan state from 1614 until 1620. Rick closed the book and folded his hands.

Looking at the other two he whispered, "Do you think that *Enrique de la Casa de Sangre* became *Don Enrique Cortez?*"

"It appears that way," Jim said, pondering the question, "but how could he have become accepted into society so quickly?"

"You have to remember that there was no such thing as criminal background checks back then," Rick said. "They couldn't just hop over to the sheriff's office and look him up in the National Crime Computer or send a request to Interpol. He just simply appeared out of nowhere and bought his way into society. Since nobody could Google his name, he was able to slip in without suspicion. Remember the book we had to read, *The Count of Monte Cristo?* He was able to do it."

"He would still have to present papers of some sort," Raúl said. "Even showing up with money and jewels, he would have to be authenticated in order to own land, but there may be a way of finding that out as well. There's one more stop that we need to make."

They returned the journal to the librarian's desk and rushed out the door to the *museo historía de Yucatan* three blocks away. Unlike the natural history museum, this one dealt with the history of the political, social, and commercial advances of the Yucatan. As with the other library, they went to the librarian who showed them where to look.

Researching the name Don Enrique Cortez, they discovered nothing except that Don Cortez appeared to have come out of nowhere. At that time he presented papers linking him to a family of rich landowners in Madrid. The family name Cortez was well known and respected. The boys also learned that some historians since have questioned the authenticity of those papers.

Don Cortez was reported to be a man of incredible wealth, and soon held titles to much land in the Yucatan. Through shrewd land acquisitions and wise business transactions, Don Cortez increased his wealth and, in the process, bought himself the governorship. From there he carved his way into the history books, though historians had never truly authenticated the source of his wealth. The boys discussed it most of the afternoon. They felt they knew how Don Cortez became wealthy without paying the price for his riches. It appeared that he had started out in life as *Enrique de la Casa de Sangre* and then became a murderous pirate.

At four o'clock the boys left the library to meet Raúl's father. *Señor* Galante had some additional news for them. "Pastor Jiménez inspected the construction site at the church today and the storm did more damage than we anticipated. The site is soaked and will have to be drained and allowed to dry out before any further assessment can be made. That will take about two or three days, so he called and reported there would be no work on the church tomorrow."

When they received the news of the cancelled work day, the boys decided it would be the perfect opportunity to take another ride to the area that the pirates and the locals nicknamed Superstition Cove. They soon found out there was to be no return trip to the cove the next day or any other day, as other activities would divert their attention in other directions.

Since the rest of the week was free, Pastor Jiménez and Ted arranged for the girls to be taken to the Galante's house for a swimming party on Wednesday. The boys were to visit a local gym.

From the outside, the building didn't appear to be anything special, just a sand-colored stucco building with a huge picture window and the name *el gimnasio de boxeo del Toro* painted on it. Through the dusty window the boys could see twenty or thirty boys and men, each working out at different stations.

Once inside, they discovered there were three boxing rings with men crowded around one of them watching two boxers sparring. The men cheered and screamed instructions at the two fighters. One boxer wore red trunks while the other blue. The boxer in blue was stockier with well-defined muscles. Rick watched as the smaller fighter jabbed and punched around his bigger opponent. Every time the larger man in blue attempted to trap his opponent in the corner, the smaller fighter jabbed and danced his way out of trouble.

Rick admired the way the smaller fighter handled the larger one, but he began feeling out of place as he glanced around the gym and noticed a weight area with the barbells and dumbbells. There were some boys doing curls and dead lifts, and another lying on a bench, pushing weights up and down. Each of the boys was lathered in sweat, and Rick felt insecure with his own body as he noticed the definition of the boys' chests and biceps from pumping iron. Several men, working out with them, wore shirts with the words *el gimnasio de boxeo del Toro* stretched tightly across their chests. Rick began to think this wasn't such a great idea after all.

Looking around, Rick also noticed the heavy bags and the speed bags. He had never used any of them before, though he had seen them in movies. He felt intimidated at the prospect of trying them out for the first time in front of his friends as well as strangers.

Pastor Jiménez introduced the boys to Umberto del Toro, a former North American light middleweight champ. *Señor* Toro was about Jim's height, but had about thirty pounds of solid muscle over the youth from the states. He wore grey sweat pants and a black tee-shirt with letters that read, "Everlast."

Señor Toro led them to the locker room and told them to change clothes. The boys were assigned lockers with gear already laid out for them. Terrell and Marcus eagerly grabbed the trunks, talking excitedly as they dressed. Rick noticed that Ken didn't seem too eager about the prospects of exercising with the rest either but began changing when he saw Jim and Rick undressing.

When they all returned to the gym, señor Toro assigned various boxers to work with each of them. Juan had been given the task of working with Jim and Rick, and Rick thought he detected a slight sneer on the teen's face as he learned of his assignment. Juan led them to the weight area where he had Rick lay down on the weight bench.

Juan said, "I'm going to warm you up on weights before you and I step in the ring."

Rick gulped and prepared himself for what was to come.

Chapter Nine

Pastor Jiménez' Confession

The older teen started by putting a hundred and twenty pounds on the bars with a cruel grin as he did so. "You should be able to press your own weight. How much do you weigh?"

"A hundred and twenty-five pounds," Rick answered.

"This should not be too hard then," the pastor's son said, smirking slightly as he finished mounting the weights onto the bar.

Rick thought he heard a small challenge in Juan's voice as the pastor's son lowered the weight onto Rick. He grabbed the bar with his hands, placing them evenly with his shoulders, and pushed with all his might. It may have only weighed a hundred and twenty pounds, but to Rick, who had never lifted weights before, it felt like the entire building was laying on top of him. After lifting it twice, he couldn't raise the bar again and was barely to keep the weight from crushing him. Rick strained beneath the overwhelming pressure for almost a minute before Juan offered relief. Rick caught a glimpse of a smile on the pastor's son's face as he lifted the bar from Rick's chest.

"Man, I thought you were tough," Juan said, taunting Rick. "You are weaker than my cousin, and she is only eight." He started laughing cruelly as he motioned for Rick to get up.

Rick blushed from embarrassment as he rolled off the bench. Even though he had never lifted weights, he knew a person had to work their way up gradually before they would be able to lift his or her own body weight. He also knew that a novice was rarely able to do it the first time. There were also breathing techniques, though Rick didn't know what they were, and that Juan failed to go over with them before they began, but rather than responding to Juan's baiting, Rick remained silent.

Juan appeared unmoved by Rick's silence. Ignoring the group's leader, he turned to Jim and said, "Here, you try it."

Jim laid on the bench. Juan removed thirty pounds of weight off the bar and lowered it onto Jim. Jim lifted the bar ten times before placing it back onto the pins with Juan's help.

Juan, still smirking, looked at Rick and said, "I will have you try something else." He led him to one of the rings where he had one of the trainers fit Rick with gloves and headgear. Breaking out a new mouth guard, the trainer gave it to Rick and helped him step through the ropes and into the ring.

On the other side of the ring, Juan parted the ropes and stepped through them. "This will only be a light sparring," Juan said as he crossed the ring.

Rick's arms felt like Jell-O and the gloves seemed as heavy as cement, but he raised them to a boxing stance anyway. He was amazed at how fast the first jab came. It snapped his head back on impact. He didn't even see the second or the third one; he only felt them. When Juan hit him in the stomach, it knocked the breath out of him, not that he noticed, because the uppercut that followed knocked him out cold.

One of the trainers that had been watching the fight entered the ring and held a bottle of smelling salts under Rick's nose. Rick woke with his vision groggy and his jaw feeling like it was about to fall off.

Pastor Jiménez came rushing over to the ring, his face flushed volcanic red as he glared at his son. "Juan, what are you doing?" he said, spatting the words out in a staccato fashion, His voice seemed to grow louder and harsher with each word. "I entrusted you with these two because I thought you would be the best one for them. You know he is no match for you in the ring. And you know better than to put him on the weight bench and then put him in the ring. You deliberately set him up to embarrass him."

The intensity of Juan's stare matched his father's as the teen glared back in pure anger. It allowed Rick to see the family resemblance between the two men.

"Put him with someone else then," Juan said, throwing his gloves down and stomping away, but before he got out of the ring he pointed at an almost unconscious Rick and said, "There is your pitiful little champion from the states." He rolled his eyes throwing his right hand into the air in disgust as he turned and said, "I am out of here." With that the dark-haired teen strode toward the locker room.

Señor Toro helped Rick up from the mat. Rick shook his head a few times before he knew where he was as the pastor helped him out of the ring.

"I am sorry, Rick," Pastor Jiménez apologized. "I do not know what gets into him."

He called for one of the trainers to bring some liniment oil. The trainer began applying it to Rick's arms, slowly massaging his biceps. "You know, you are in fairly good shape for not lifting weights. Do you play any other sports?"

Rick thought the man was just being kind, but when he looked him in the eyes he sensed the man's sincerity. The pastor smiled warmly as gentle wrinkles creased the corners of his brown eyes.

"I play baseball and basketball. I'd like to play football, but my school doesn't have a team."

"Good. It is good that you play team sports. It is important for boys to be involved in group activities. They learn to function well with others. I got Juan started in boxing, which is not a group sport. He excels at it, as I did, but as a result, he sometimes does not work well with others. Occasionally he will help some of the other boys in the gym, but that is all. It is because of boxing that I have been able to win fourteen young men to the Lord. Three of them are in the ministry today." He looked away as if viewing something from a distance, then he hung his head slightly.

"It sounds like there's more to the story," Rick said as he began flexing his arms.

"Twenty some years ago I was the middleweight champ of Guerrero." The pastor's voice dwindled to a mere whisper. "No one could stay in the ring with me for more than three rounds. I was untouchable. Many of my friends and other boxers told me that I should turn pro, but I ignored them. That year I tried out for my country's Olympic team. For the first time, I came up against boxers who were as good, if not better, than I was. I became the runner-up in all of Mexico and the first alternate for the Olympic team in my weight class. The champion got injured just before the Olympics and I represented my country in Los Angeles. The Soviets did not come that year, and many of the athletes were happy about that. I won the bronze, and returned to my country a hero, and for that I received a hero's welcome. Everywhere I went, there were celebrations in my honor."

He paused, reflecting on the memory, and laughed as if enjoying a private joke. Snapping out of his reverie he said, "How do your arms feel, Rick?"

"Better," Rick said, flexing his arms. "They feel much better. Thank you."

"Good," the pastor said. "I will put you on the speed bag. It is less demanding physically. I do not wish to risk any more damage to you. Thank you, Carlos," he added as he nodded to the trainer. "That will be all for now."

They crossed to the other side of the gym where the speed bags hung. As they passed one of the rings, Rick watched Terrell and Marcus sparring. Terrell's soft cast was at this point more for show than necessity. With the gloves on their fists and wearing the safety headgear, the twins weaved and bobbed, jabbing at each other lightly, encouraged by the cheers of other fighters watching from outside the ring.

"What was it like to be famous?" Rick asked.

Pastor Jiménez appeared to ignore the question as he began his demonstration of the speed bag. First, he explained to them that the bag should be level with their chin. Then he stood with his feet shoulder length apart and square with the bag. Holding his fists near chin level, he struck the bag.

"If you noticed, I did not hit the bag with my knuckles, but rather, I hit it with the side of my fist. That is not a good fighting technique, but the purpose of the speed bag is to develop your hand-eye coordination. Relax. Do not get tense; just let the bag do the work."

He struck the bag again. "Did you notice that I brought my fist back into a position immediately? You should hit it with one fluid motion. Strike and bring it back. Listen to the bag. After an odd number of rebounds, you can strike the bag again. It should be coming toward you, and you should strike it while it is at about a forty-five-degree angle away from you."

He started slowly at first, both hands moving together fluidly like pistons as they struck the leather. Gradually, he increased his speed until the bag appeared to be nothing more than a blur.

"The celebrations were wonderful," he said, stopping the bag and returning to the original subject. He adjusted he bag to Jim's height. "Someone suggested that if I had won the gold I could have been elected president. I do not know about that, but I was instantly popular, and I failed miserably at handling it."

Jim struck the bag and began a rhythm, making syncopated sounds as the bag slapped against the boards. Pastor Jiménez watched to make sure Jim was getting the hang of it and then sat on a bench beside Rick. "I learned that you can measure a man's character not by how he handles adversity, but how he handles success. I could not say no to the gifts, to the flattery, and most of all to the women. I led a fast lifestyle, the kind that most young men dream about, but there was a terrible price to pay. The Bible is correct when it says that the wages of sin is death. My lifestyle soon took its toll, and before long I had lost my competitive edge. In order to regain it, I became desperate and turned to drugs."

Pastor Jiménez stopped Jim and put Rick in front of the bag, again showing him a simple rhythm. Then he showed him how to switch hands.

"Don't worry about speed as much as rhythm. Just make your movements even and natural."

As Rick took his first tentative strokes, Pastor Jiménez continued his story.

"My drug habit became so demanding that I almost sold my Olympic bronze medal for a fix. I was on my way to a pawn shop when I met a Christian who was passing out tracts. I had never been witnessed to before, and I did not know what to think. He handed me a tract, which I took with me. A month before that I would have laughed in his face, but the Lord knew I was ready. The man asked me if I was empty inside. I almost hit the man, but instead I fought back the tears and ran home like a scared little school girl. It felt as if he had been reading my mail and knew everything about me, but how could he?

"At home I took the tract out of my pocket and began reading it. The words seemed to burn a hole in my heart. It asked me if I was saved and ready for eternity. It went on to name many of the sins that were holding me in bondage. As I read it, I started crying. I wept for hours. I could not stop. I cried until I thought I there were no more tears left in me. When I stopped, I felt completely drained. But then I read the rest of the tract. It told me that Jesus would fill all the voids in my life that drugs and alcohol had created. Even though I had been raised a Catholic, I prayed that night for the first time in my life.

"The next day, I visited the church and spoke with the pastor. Together we prayed and I accepted Christ. I was baptized and within a month I felt a call to the ministry and enrolled in the Bible College. That was where I met my future wife, Juanita.

"I thought Boxing had given me everything that I valued in life and then it took it away, but the truth is serving the Lord has given me all that I ever needed. Only now, I fear that Boxing may have taken the one thing I cherish most; my son."

The bag sputtered as Rick missed it. He stopped the bag to start over, but before he struck the bag he said to the minister, "Maybe you haven't lost him. Maybe he just hasn't found that place where God is more important to him than anything else. Maybe that will come."

Rick started the speed bag again, this time falling easily into a gentle rhythm. *Thunka-chunka, thunka-chunka, thunka-chunka.*

"You may be only fourteen, but you are wiser than your years," the pastor said.

Rick began chuckling. "I think Ted would disagree with you about that."

"I think Ted is more impressed with you than you think." He watched Rick striking the bag and encouraged him. "That is a good rhythm. You have picked this up very quick."

The pastor hesitated for a moment, as if he was searching for the right words.

"Help me pray for Juan," he pled. "He may seem antagonistic toward you, but I can tell he respects you. He has heard about your group and how it started. He heard how you aided the police, but I guess he did not know what to expect. In part, it is my fault. I built up your group so much to the church I guess maybe he expected every one of you to be over seven feet tall. In the long run, it is probably best that he sees what great things can be accomplished by just ordinary people."

Thunka-chunka, thunka-chunka, thunka-chunka. Rick stopped hitting the bag and turned to the minister. "I'll tell you what, if you promise not to tell the girls how bad I am at boxing, we'll make Juan a mission project while we're down here."

Pastor Jiménez laughed. "You are a lot better at boxing than I was the first time I tried it, but you have a deal. I think Juan would like for you to reach out to him. Thank you."

They finished on the heavy bag, and Rick understood immediately how it got its name. Rick and Jim were finishing up and gathering their gear when they heard a commotion coming from the middle ring. About a dozen men were standing outside the ring watching two fighters sparring. When Rick looked again, he was surprised to discover one of the fighters was Raúl. What was even more astonishing was the other fighter was Ken.

Chapter Ten
Ken and Kim Shine

Rick watched Raúl weave and bob around Ken, stalking him like a hunter tracking his prey. Jabbing as he moved, Raúl tested the larger opponent. He crouched low, his hands up and close to his face. A lather of perspiration dampened him, glistening off his brown skin as he moved and jabbed, working his way around the ring. From his stance, Rick could tell he had been well trained, probably by Juan or Pastor Jiménez personally. He circled Ken, moving clockwise around the taller opponent, throwing small jabs every once in a while, keeping Ken off balance and forcing him to back up.

At first Raúl's punches found their mark, even though Ken balanced himself on the back of his heels in order to stay away from the ferocious unrelenting jabs. Like a cat toying with a mouse, Raúl continued pursuing Ken, circling and punching. One to the chin, another to the ribs, another to the jaw. With each hit, Ken appeared more and more stunned as Raúl continued punishing him while the crowd of men cheered him on.

Sensing a strong finish was imminent, Raúl moved in closer. He feinted to his right and jabbed again with his left. To everyone watching it appeared that Ken was just going through the motions, taking the hits with little effort to stop them, until Ken changed tactics. As Raúl dropped his right shoulder to jab once again, Ken changed to a left-handed boxing stance. A right hander by nature, Ken shifted from his natural style of leading with his left to that of a southpaw, leading with his right. Raúl's jab missed, but the left side of his face was wide open. Ken threw a right jab to the side of Raúl's face, tagging and stunning his more experienced opponent. The change in tactic confused

Raúl who suddenly found himself on the defense as Ken began pummeling him with one jab after another.

Ken began circling Raúl, turning the tables on his younger opponent and moving counter clockwise against the more experienced fighter. The crowd, awed by the change in tactic, began encouraging Ken with their cheers and shouts. Raúl tried stepping away, but every time he moved, Ken countered, peppering him with even more right jabs.

With Raúl against the ropes, Ken switched up once again. Raúl's eyes opened wide, and for a moment he seemed revived, adjusting to Ken's left jab. Ken jabbed twice with his left hand, clearly on the offensive, and both times Raúl blocked the advances with his right arm. Ken shuffled his feet, faked a left jab, and as Raúl's arm came up, Ken threw an uppercut to Raúl's chin.

Raúl's head whipped back under the force and before he could react, Ken hit him again with a one-two combination, sending the younger fighter crashing to the canvass. The gym was filled with the shouts of admiration as the spectator's around the ring howled their appreciation for a good fight. The white of his mouthpiece could be seen as Ken grinned, amused at all the attention he was receiving. Reaching down, he helped Raúl to his feet, placing an arm around the shoulder of the younger opponent as they left the ring together. Several fighters slapped Ken on the back in admiration, complimenting him on a good fight. Even though the men spoke in Spanish, he could tell they were cheering for him.

After their showers, the boys returned to the bus. Rick sat beside Raúl.

"How was it?" Rick said.

"I enjoyed it very much. Of course, I come here often, but it was wonderful sharing the gym with you guys. Ken surprised me," he continued. "He is so smart and he catches on so quickly that I was afraid. After only a few minutes, he was using techniques that I had not even thought of. He told me he watched the other fighters around the gym, studied what they were doing, and then after letting me hit on him for about five minutes, he started using what he had learned in order to beat me. I have never seen a fighter adjust so quickly in my life. I could tell Pastor Jiménez was impressed as well."

"I know what you mean," Rick said smiling and looking at Ken who was sitting in the back with Terrell. He figured they were talking about the fight, knowing that Terrell had been watching with fascination. "He scares us too. When we get to the church, we need to talk to Ken and Kim before they get away."

Ken caught Rick's eyes after hearing his name. He knew something was happening and nodded slightly to Rick without alerting any of the others. In spite of Ken's subtlety, both Rick and Jim knew it was time to let the rest of the Ten in on their mystery. By the time the guys returned from the gym, the girls had already arrived at the church and the workers had left for the day. The two women that Mackenzie and Wendy were staying with were there to pick them up, but none of the others had arrived yet.

Rick, Raúl, and Jim cornered Kim and Ken in the sanctuary and told them about the chest, leaving out the part of the break-in. Then they talked about their discovery at the grotto.

"That rock fell for about two seconds before we heard the splash," Rick said. "Do you have any idea how far it dropped?"

"Well," Ken said, adjusting his glasses, "there are several variables that must be factored in. The first is the weight of the rock itself. The second is how much wind resistance…"

"Earth to Ken," Rick said with more than a little impatience, "how about a ballpark figure?"

Ken looked at Kim with a smile on his face. She pulled a small tablet and a pencil from her purse and began writing furiously as the boy's talked. Ken began explaining what she was doing.

"Kim's working on the formula for velocity," he said. "It's fairly simple. The easiest formula is thirty-two feet per second per second. That's what Kim's doing right now. Although there *are* other factors that have to be taken into consideration if you really want to know the force with which the object hits the water."

Jim, who was not exactly a dummy in science, looked at Ken like he was explaining quantum physics and black hole or string theories.

"Ken, just pretend that we didn't just fly in from another planet and only barely understand eighth grade science. How far did it drop?"

Kim finished with the calculations and said, "About sixty-four feet. Maybe a little less, but either way, you would run a huge risk if you fell. You'd drop sixteen feet the first second, but with your acceleration, in another second, you'd travel sixty feet. In three seconds, you'd hit the water one hundred and forty feet below where you started.

"Think of it like this; everything we do generates some kind of energy. A sneeze, a cough, a slap on the back; they all create energy. These seem harmless, and they are, until that energy is directed against us. Suppose your timing was off. The old *one potato one — two potato two* method is sadly inaccurate. Let's say you started the count thee tenths of a second late. You counted your potatoes but your count was slightly slower than it should have been. If you ran track, in three seconds you would be at the five-yard line, the twenty-yard line, and then the fifty. You would finish the hundred-meter dash in about four and a half seconds. Hitting the water at that distance and at that speed, you could shatter every bone in your body if you were lucky. You'd smack the water at a pressure of about a hundred pounds per square inch. All of your internal organs would be torn loose. At the same time, your ribs would splinter, sending shards of cartilage into your lungs, your liver, and even your heart."

"You'll be moving at about eighty miles per hour when you collide with the water. You'd be like the Flash," Ken added sarcastically, "and you wouldn't need the Jupiter mafia to try and kill you, because you'd do it yourself."

Rick knew the reference was concerning the night that he spent in the Johnson's back yard with Terrell and Marcus, the night before their adventure at the mall and Marcus' night in the graveyard.

"That's not going to happen to us," Rick said, "because we're going to use rope and we're going to be careful."

Ken and Kim knew they didn't have to remind Rick about Marcus's experience in the graveyard or the slight altercation at Rick's house, in which a lamp, an end table, and a coffee table got smashed and a window got broken. There was also the matter of Terrell's broken arm. They knew that the words *Rick* and *careful* were rarely used in the same sentence except as a warning.

"If you should fall from the rope and only drop for half a second, you would end up breaking your back when you hit the water," Ken warned.

The boys fell silent. They had never thought about what would happen if the rope snapped. Finally, Rick added, "But if we don't try, we'll never know for sure."

Señor Galante arrived to pick them up, so Rick left with Raúl and Jim, leaving the Walker teens wondering if he was really foolhardy enough to try going down into the grotto, and hoping that he wasn't.

The next day, the boys once again helped with the foundation, picking up what the backhoe had left behind. In the afternoon, the rain returned, stopping the work. The cement was to be poured the next day and the carpenters were scheduled to arrive Monday to frame the new building after the cement dried over the weekend. As the rain began, the boys hurried to cover the wood with tarps. Tropical Storm Clayton, on the heels of Beverly, had only managed sustained winds of forty miles per hour and already had begun losing intensity, but the rain was still enough to delay the work for the day, even though the heaviest downpour only lasted twenty minutes. With five hours to kill until Raúl's father would arrive to pick them up, the boys thought it was a great opportunity to return to the Historical Museum of the Yucatan. For two hours they went through old land grants and purchases, starting with the year 1609. The records showed that in March of 1610, Don Cortez began purchasing over a hundred thousand acres during a period of two years. His real estate holdings were scattered throughout the Yucatan. During those two years he had become one of the richest men in the Peninsula. Then, just as suddenly, around September of 1612, he began selling his holdings for incredible profits. They were surprised to discover that Don Cortez donated a parcel of land to the Order of Franciscan Monks in 1617. It was the same plot of land that the church sat on.

"So," Jim said, "the murderer and plunderer became a philanthropist. But why, I wonder, did he start selling off his holdings? Was his contribution to the church for absolution?"

Though they still lacked answers, after four hours they left, arriving just in time to meet with *Señor* Galante. On the way home, Raúl's father told them that Saturday the church had a picnic planned, with a softball game afterwards. With the contribution from The Ten, the lumber and labor for the new building was now paid for. Their portion of the labor was complete, so for the next week-and-a-half Pastor Jiménez was going to share with them his work with the Mayan people. They would be leaving for a trip into the jungle on Tuesday. Rick hoped it wouldn't interfere with their current adventure which (along with his promise to Pastor Jiménez concerning Juan) had now become the group's real mission work.

Chapter Eleven

A Familiar Game

On Saturday morning, Pastor Jiménez and Ted held a brief meeting with the group, discussing their itinerary for the week.

"Several years ago," Pastor Jiménez began, "I was able to establish an opening into the Mayan community. God opened the door for me and has allowed me to go at least once a month ever since. I have found them to be a very industrious and honest people, but they are somewhat reclusive and aloof. I hope all of you appreciate what a wonderful opportunity it is for all of you to observe them in their natural habitat.

"Before we arrive at the Mayan colony," he continued, "I have contracted my guide. He will lead us on a five-day excursion through the Yucatan. We will see some of the Mayan ruins as well as many of the beautiful ecological wonders the Yucatan has to share."

He turned to Ted and asked, "Do you know how many in your group can swim?"

Ted called for a show of hands and everyone raised their hands, although Terrell knew he wouldn't be allowed to go swimming because he still had a cast on his arm.

"Good, not that it would make that much difference, because all of you will be given snorkeling lessons the third day. That is so you can truly enjoy the beauty of the grottos."

Jim turned his head quickly to catch a glimpse of Rick and Raúl's reaction. Rick, with a crooked grin on his face, looked like a kid who just heard he was going to the circus. His eyes twinkled as he thought about the trip and how it would help him understand the grotto system better. At the same time, his breathing sped up slightly thinking about the treasure.

Wendy, sitting beside Juan, arched her eyebrows and eyed him suspiciously, noticing Rick's reaction to the news. Rick gave her a candid smile but then turned his attention back to Pastor Jiménez. He knew Wendy was miffed, but he wasn't ready to let everyone in on the secret just yet, and besides, if she was that interested in him, she wouldn't be sitting with Juan.

Following the meeting, the group was taken to a nearby park where the church had prepared a large picnic. The group was treated to the usual picnic fare of hamburgers and hot dogs, but there was also plenty of Mexican food to satisfy everyone.

After the meal, they went to a nearby softball diamond. Ted and Pastor Jiménez chose sides dividing the group into two teams. Pastor Jiménez chose Rick, Juan, Wendy, Marcus, and Kim as well as three boys and a girl from his church. Ted had Jim, Raúl, Mackenzie, Ken, Terrell, and two girls and two boys, also from the church.

Rick played centerfield so he could help cover right field where Kim was placed. Wendy played second base, which she seemed to enjoy since it was next to first base where Juan was playing. Watching both of them, Rick hoped she could keep her eyes off the preacher's son long enough to catch the ball if it was hit to her.

The first three innings passed without incident except for the three errors committed by Wendy. Rick felt one was genuine, but two of them he could have sworn was because her head was turned to the left at the wrong time. Ted's team soon picked up the idea that if they hit it in her direction they would have a better chance to get on base. It wasn't an automatic hit, but it was close enough of a sure thing that the boys began hitting it her way on purpose. Rick counteracted their strategy by moving their team's short fielder directly behind Wendy as a backup. She still missed several balls, but the short fielder was able to throw out two of the batters before they reached first base and prevent other base runners from scoring.

In the fourth inning, with two outs, the batter hit a short pop-up to short centerfield. Rick raced for the ball, charging forward as it started to drop. Attempting a sliding catch, Rick learned the hard way that sliding in a dirt outfield wasn't as easy as sliding in grass. His right foot caught on a rock and instead of sliding he tumbled head over heel. When he stopped rolling, he tried standing but tumbled again, as the ball bounced past him. The batter made it to second and the game was halted while Pastor Jiménez and Ted checked to see if Rick was alright. Rick sat up to view the damage. The worst was his blue jeans, which now had a hole torn in the right knee. He imagined how his mother would react to that and cringed more from that than the pain. If she added the cost of new jeans to his already insurmountable debt caused by the damage from their altercation with the two thieves, he wouldn't see a dime of allowance until Thanksgiving.

"Can you bend your leg?" Ted asked as he examined the damage.

Rick bent his right leg, winced slightly from the pain, and said, "It hurts a little, but I'll be alright."

"Are you sure, son?" Pastor Jiménez said. "It appears to be scraped pretty bad."

"I may regret it in the morning," Rick said, "because it'll be sore, but I think it'll be okay."

The pastor held out his hand to help Rick up. "You have a lot of *machismo*, Rick."

As everyone returned to their positions, Wendy lingered. "Are you really okay?" she asked. Her green eyes scanned him for potential damage, but Rick could tell by her face that she was genuinely concerned.

"Yes. It's a little sore, but I'm alright."

"I'm glad," she said, her tone taking on a breathy quality. "We haven't had much time to talk since arriving two weeks ago. Hopefully we can spend some time together on the camping trip."

She turned and ran back to her position without saying another word.

Rick watched her, his affection for her overshadowing what he had been feeling for almost two weeks. He felt like reminding her that all of her free time since they arrived in Mexico had been spent with Juan but decided it best not to mention it. He jogged back stiff-legged to his place in centerfield to continue the game.

At the bottom of the seventh inning, the agreed upon length for the game, Rick's team prepared to take their final at bats with Ted's team leading 14 − 11, leaving Rick's team needing three runs to tie and four to win. Marcus batted first and hit a double. Kim followed him by hitting a ground ball directly to the first baseman for the first out. Juan tried to blast the ball to outer space, but missing most of it, succeeding only in hitting a grounder to the third baseman. Instead of throwing Juan out at first, the boy held the ball in order to prevent Marcus from moving up. Next, Wendy slapped the ball to short right field and the bases were loaded with Rick coming to bat.

The Mariners are in position to win the World Series. Rick Barber's teammates have loaded the bases and all he has to do is deliver the death blow. One mighty swing of the bat and history will be made.

Barber purposely takes his time getting to the plate. The crowd is on their feet. The noise level is deafening, but to a consummate professional like Barber it's as natural as a walk in the park.

He stands in the box, dangles his bat lazily in his right hand, and lifting his left arm, points to a spot in centerfield. The crowd cheers even louder. They are beside themselves. Visions of the great Bambino himself, Babe Ruth, has the crowd in a frenzy fit. Everyone knows there will be celebrations in the streets tonight.

The ball is pitched, a slow floater that arcs and drifts gently to the plate. Barber tenses, shifts his feet, and...

...smacked the ball with all his might toward right field.

Mackenzie turned and gave chase to the ball as it flew past, well over her head. Marcus scored, and Juan after him. Mackenzie retrieved the ball as Rick rounded second. She attempted to throw the ball, but it slipped from her hand so, by the time she retrieved it again, Wendy was able to score. Mackenzie got the ball to Jim who turned to throw it to home plate. By that time, Rick had turned the corner at third, but with his poor leg, he was reduced to only three-quarter speed. Common sense should have dictated for Rick to hold up, but adrenaline overrode any commands that logic was giving. He was most of the way to home plate when the ball hopped past Raúl and bounded all the way to the backstop. By the time the young catcher grabbed it, Rick had crossed the plate with the winning run and crashed to the ground when his injured leg buckled under the stress.

Rick's team ran to greet him and the first to reach him, to Rick's surprise, was Juan. The pastor's son had a smile on his face that spread from cheek to cheek as he lifted Rick off the ground. There was no way to mistake his smile as anything but pure pleasure.

"That was a great hit, Rick," Juan said. He turned and walked away as the others gathered and came between him and Rick.

Rick felt that something had shifted between him and Juan. It was as if pieces of a wall had begun to crumble. He felt warm inside from the thought that he had broken through, and in a small way had made progress toward reaching Juan. He knew it wasn't much, but it was a start, like a small stream eroding a boulder. It doesn't happen all at once, but eventually the water running over the stone will gradually eat away at it until it's gone. He thanked God for the sign and, if that was what it was, he could work with it. With the help of God, the start would be sufficient and the wall between them, just like the ones at Jericho, would come crashing down.

Chapter Twelve
A Face that doesn't Belong

At 8:00 on Tuesday morning the group gathered at the church, anxious about the opportunity to witness the work being done among the Mayan people. Having heard about it for almost a year, several of the members had taken the time to read about the Mayan Empire. The history of the ancient race went almost as far back as the birth of Christ. Excitement had been running deeply though the group ever since they knew the trip was to take place a year earlier than originally planned. The anticipation grew even more as the day neared. Accompanying the group was Alfonso, acting as a chaperone, since many of the parents were not able to get away for the entire eight-day excursion.

Pastor Jiménez introduced their guide to the group. "This is Luis Peron. *Señor* Peron is a professional guide with over twenty years of experience. I have asked him to address the group and fill you in on what you can expect."

Señor Peron was taller than most of his countrymen with lean muscular features. His dark complexion was enhanced by a thin mustache. He was dressed in khaki pants and a simple polo shirt. As he explained the tour, he also spoke to them about what he expected from each of them. Rick recognized the man, having seen him at the church service the previous Sunday. As he spoke to the rest of the group, Rick, Jim, Raúl, and Juan loaded the bus.

"I see that most of the girls and several of the boys are wearing shorts. That is fine for the northern part of the peninsula, but after day three, I will caution you to wear long pants. When we get to the Sian Ka'an Biosphere Reservation, you will not want to wear shorts in the jungle. Also, it is important to wear mosquito repellant and sun screen at all times. The mosquitoes can be terrible in this region and you have already learned about the dangers of our sun. I do not wish to return a week from now with a group of extra-crispy, disease-infected tourists."

The group laughed at the obvious humor, though some of them noticed Marcus's eyes growing large at the mention of diseases, adding one more item to his ever-growing list of things to be feared.

After they were quiet again, *señor* Peron continued. "The Yucatan Peninsula is made up of three of Mexico's states; Yucatan, Quintana Roo, and Campeche. We will be traveling through all three. You will also find that we will pass from one state to the next freely, much like you do in your country.

"Our itinerary is going to be very busy. This morning we will stop at Chichen Itza, the most famous of the Mayan ruins. We will arrive around ten o'clock, but we will only be able to spend a few hours there because we do not wish to spend too much time in the Yucatan sun, so by two o'clock we will be back on the tour bus and traveling toward the coast. That is where we will spend the night. I can finish this briefing on the bus, which should be just about loaded with the equipment we will need, so I suggest we get moving."

The church's bus was a twenty-four passenger Bluebird with air conditioning. The boys had just finished loading the gear and luggage when the group began climbing onto the bus. Pastor Jiménez watched as the group carefully, noticing Juan and Rick working together. He caught Rick's eye and nodded slightly while smiling his approval.

Juan made small talk with the other three as the group boarded. Rick felt it was an attempt on Juan's part to reach out to Jim and himself. Before stepping onto the bus, Rick caught a glimpse of León peeking around the corner of the church. He had been eavesdropping and heard *señor* Peron's description of their trip. Not that it would matter, Rick thought, since only the first day had been discussed, but it still bothered him knowing that León had been listening. He was going to mention it to Jim and Raúl, but it was probably nothing to be concerned about.

Juan sat in the driver's seat and Rick and Wendy in the first seat behind him. Across the aisle from them sat the pastor and Luis, with Ted and Brenda behind them. Behind Rick sat Mackenzie and Jim. The others paired up as the bus got underway.

When they left the city limits of Mérida, Luis stood in the middle of the aisle and continued his speech.

"On day two, we will visit Isla Contoy in Quintana Roo. The island is a refuge for over sixty different species of marine birds, some of them very rare. Day three will be spent on Isla Cozumel, where you will receive snorkeling lessons. This will come in handy when we visit the grottos."

Wendy stole a glance at Rick, but his face was a mask of non-commitment. She still hadn't talked to him about her suspicions concerning his reaction to the word grotto.

Luis walked a little further up the aisle and continued talking as he went. "Day four is when you will need to be concerned. We will be visiting the reservation. It will be important, for you own protection, that you stay with the group at all times while we are in the interior. It is one of the most beautiful places in the world, but it can also be one of the most deadly."

From out of the corner of his eye, Rick could see Ted staring at him. He smiled in spite of wondering what Ted was thinking.

"At all times, remember that you are in a wilderness. There are a variety of wild cats and poisonous snakes, and unfortunately, they don't know that you're only tourists. To the jaguar you're lunch, and to the boa constrictor just another intruder into his world."

Rick didn't know if the purpose of señor Peron's talk was to frighten the group, but if it was, he was succeeding. He slowly panned the group and saw that he had gotten the attention of several in the group, and for once it wasn't just Marcus who was alarmed.

"I do not wish to scare you unnecessarily, because the number of people killed on these reservations is very low, but it does happen. Most of the cats are nocturnal, and they avoid man whenever possible, but if you come across them unexpectedly it would be most unfortunate, because even the Little Spotted Cat can be extremely dangerous, if not deadly."

Rick could tell from the collective expressions of the group that two things had been accomplished. The first was *señor* Peron had their undivided attention, and the second was that he had them sufficiently concerned.

"I can tell all of you from experience that trouble comes to most tourists because they think they are perfectly safe. I want to make sure that you don't treat this like it's a trip to *Six Flags over the Yucatan*, because it is not.

"On day five we will be in Bacalar where we will visit Laguna Bacalar and *la laguna de los siete colores*, or in your language, The Lagoon of Seven Colors. When you get there, you will understand where it gets its name. It will prove, no doubt, to be one of the most beautiful sites you will see on this trip, if not your lifetime. It is internationally famous and one of the most incredible places in the entire world.

"That night, you will be in a church service with some Mayan people. Pastor Jiménez has been working with this group for over two years now. It is where I first met him, and where I received the Lord. Since then we have made the trip together at least once a month. The rest of the trip will be spent at Calakmul in Campache, and then on to Punta Put and finally the Rio Celestun Biosphere Reservation in the Yucatan. While you will experience a lot, it would not even be one hundredth of all that the Yucatan has to offer, but it will be a most memorable journey nonetheless."

The bus arrived at Chichen Itza just before eleven o'clock. Luis divided the group so that half the group went with him and the other

THE SECRET OF SUPERSTITION COVE

with Pastor Jiménez. Raúl and Juan were in Luis' group with Rick and Jim.

Before the groups separated, Ted took Rick and Jim aside for a talk. Although his expression appeared normal, there was a sternness in his voice that Rick couldn't miss.

"Now, remember," he said, "I don't want any trouble from either of you. I don't want a repeat of the airport incident; understand?"

They both assured him that they would be on their best behavior. After all, Rick reminded him, what kind of trouble could they get into at some ruins?

For the next three hours they toured the three sections of the ruins; the North group, the Central group, and the Southern or "Old Chichen" group. Luis was very informative, explaining the Toltec styling of the Northern group and how it differed from the original Mayan architecture of the other two sections.

"The ancient Mayans used the cenotes for human sacrifices," Luis said. "In fact, the very name Chichen Itza comes from three words; chi which means mouth, *chen* which means well, and *itza* which means of the witch water. The priests would throw the human sacrifices into the cenote to please the gods, and if they lived, it was believed they were seers and held special places of honor, but, as you can imagine, seers were few and far between.

"Now before you think that is silly, think about your own history of the witch trials in Salem. They would accuse a girl, throw her in the river, and if she drowned it proved that she was not a witch. If she swam to shore, that was proof that she was a witch, because only a witch could float. When she reached the shore, she was arrested and killed for being a witch."

"How did they survive a fall like that?" Rick asked. "Isn't it a pretty big drop?"

"Certainly; most of these drops into the grottos are between fifty and ninety feet," Luis explained. "There is a technique. It will be easier for me to show you than to explain it, but basically you can do a tuck and roll. You can literally become a human cannonball. It takes a lot of the force out of the impact."

The group finally arrived at the largest of all the pyramids. "This is called *el Castillo del Serpiente Emplumado*. That means the castle of the plumed serpent. The Mayans called the serpent god *Kukulkán*. You may remember the prophecies that claimed the world would end on December 22, 2012. All the news networks carried the story. The Mayans believed the serpent god would rise from the ground of the ball court and end the world for good. But, as you can tell, that didn't happen, and because of that, it has become easier to evangelize them."

"Where's the ball court?" Jim asked.

Señor Perez gave Jim a surprised look. "How do you know about that? Are you aware of the unique qualities of the ball court?"

Jim, pleased with the praise, said, "I read about it when I learned we were going to visit the Mayan ruins."

"That is wonderful. The court is just below us." He led them down stone steps until they arrived at an immense open area, enclosed on both sides by huge observation walls.

"The Mayans held the number seven to be sacred," Luis explained as they entered the arena. "The men would play a game called pok ta pok. There were six men on each team. They were not allowed to use their hands, much like what you call soccer but we call *fútbol*. They would attempt to get the ball to their captain, the *seventh* member of the team. He would hit the ball with a racket in an attempt to put it through those rings on the walls. Those rings are precisely *seven* meters above the ground.

"The winning captain would then be beheaded, which was believed to be a great honor." Luis laughed as he viewed the shocked expressions on the faces of the group. "I believe nowadays your star athletes would prefer to be released as free agents, but that was not the case back then."

"That sounds even worse than the witch trial," Rick whispered to

Wendy. He was rewarded with the sound of her giggling, something he had not heard since they arrived.

The group looked on in amazement at the size of the arena. Rick closed his eyes. He could almost hear ancient warriors hurling their bodies at each other in an attempt to control the ball.

Luis lowered his voice to almost a whisper.

"You will notice that there is a lot of echoing down here. Can you imagine what it would have sounded like with over thirty thousand spectators screaming at the top of their lungs? Add to that the sound of athletes competing on the ball court and the noise must have been deafening. But as strange as that is to imagine, here's something else that modern scientists *still* find baffling." He turned to Wendy and asked, "What is your name?"

Wendy immediately stopped giggling. She blushed as she spoke. "Wendy."

"Okay. Listen and count the number of echoes." With that he raised his hands to his mouth like a megaphone and hollered, "Wendy."

Immediately they heard the echo say, "*Wendy, Wendy, Wendy, Wendy, Wendy, Wendy, Wendy,*" each repetition growing gradually softer than the previous one.

When it stopped, Luis asked, "How many times did it echo?"

The group was amazed; seven times. Then Luis explained that if you clap your hands it would echo exactly seven times. After that, Luis showed them carvings on the wall depicting a victorious captain after his decapitation with seven serpents growing out of his neck.

As they were leaving the ball court and moving on to the Southern section, Mackenzie thought she saw someone she had seen before. The man was at the end of the court, and standing, or so it seemed, in such a manner as to obscure his face. She tried to remember where she had seen the husky Mexican, but unable to recall, decided it was unimportant. Later, she would wish she had told someone sooner, but that would be much later, and wouldn't help the group in time.

Chapter Thirteen
A Midnight Visitor

On the second day of the trip, the group visited Isla Contoy, a small island off Cancun. *Señor* Peron explained to them the importance the island held for conservationists and the variety of species that found sanctuary there.

"This island is only about four miles long and at the widest part of the island it is only about twenty-two yards. It is really just a long strip of land in the Yucatan Channel, but it is the perfect habitat for many birds and marine animals. Permission to visit the island can only be obtained through the government."

"How did we get permission to come so quickly?" Rick asked, referring to the fact that the group only decided to make the trip a few days before they had arrived.

Luis smiled and picked up a small shell lying by his feet. He had seen Rick's type before. No matter what the subject, if he wanted an answer, he was never intimidated by the circumstances, the status of the person he was addressing, or the gravity of the subject. He would just ask and let the chips fall where they may. Luis noticed it first at the pyramids when Rick asked about the drowning of the witches at Chichen Itza. Luis knew some of the others wanted to know also, but it was Rick who waded in without hesitation. It was easy to understand why he was the leader of the group.

Luis examined the shell and then reached over and handed it to Monica.

"I set this visit up two weeks ago, when we first learned that your group would be coming this year instead of next. When I explained who you were and what your group did, the Mexican government was more than happy to grant you access to the island rather than make you wait."

They started walking the length of the island, stopping as Luis pointed out the different species of birds. Halfway across the island they came upon a group of conservationists who were roping off a section of the beach.

"What are they doing over there?" Wendy asked pointing to the scientists.

Luis looked at her. He could see why she was with Rick. She had the same sense of adventure and curiosity that he did, but with a little more self-control. It was safer to inquire about an aviary than to plunge into the machinations of a witch trial.

"They're roping off an area, and if I'm not mistaken, they're protecting a nest of sea turtle eggs," Ken answered. He began blushing when he realized everyone, including Luis, was watching him. "I saw it demonstrated on the nature channel."

"I believe you are right," said Luis. While the group waited, he walked over to one of the men, the one who appeared to be the leader, and began talking to him. After several minutes the man followed Luis back to the group.

"Hello," the man said. He took off his baseball cap that read *Pompano Beach Sea Life Rescuers.* As he did so, he wiped his brow with a handkerchief that he pulled from the back pocket of his khaki shorts. His long thin face was deeply tanned and wrinkled, and he appeared to be about fifty, however, he could have been younger but the many years in the sun and his white beard that made him appear older.

"My name is Dr. Richard Fullerton," the man in way of introduction. "We're protecting a nest of sea turtles that we expect will hatch either tonight or tomorrow. Many of the newly hatched babies have a good chance to survive due to their relatively close proximity to the water. I understand that you kids are from the states. This is a beautiful island; wouldn't you agree?"

The group replied enthusiastically, having been amazed at the natural beauty they had already observed.

"If you want," Doctor Fuller said, "I can take you over to the egg sight, but I can only escort two at a time."

Pairing off, the group took turns as Dr. Fullerton showed them the sea turtle's nest. The small plot of land had been staked out in order to keep the public away from the nest.

After leaving the area, the group walked the length of the small island, enjoying its beauty and remarking often at the variety of birds homed there, especially the ones that they had never seen before. Several Ruddy Crakes came right up to their feet, and there were flocks of White Ibises and American Flamingoes wading in the shallow waters off the shore. They observed large, exotic, wading birds with black heads, large black bills, and red rings at the base of their necks. Luis called them Jabiru Storks, and said they were a very rare breed.

Returning to the mainland, the group ate lunch before driving to Tulum. From there they took a boat to another island by the name of Isla Cozumel, where they spent four hours learning how to snorkel. As promised, Luis showed the boys the dive he spoke about at Chichen Itza. Climbing to a ledge about fifteen feet above the water, he dove off the cliff, tucked his head into his chest, and pulled his knees upward with his hands under his thighs. All of the boys tried the maneuver with varying degrees of success. Terrell was the only member of the group who didn't participate in the activities due to the cast on his arm. He spent most of the afternoon talking with Alfonso instead, and listening to the stories the old man told him about his past.

Stopping at a camping site, they were given instructions on how to set up their tents. Their campsite had shower facilities for boys and girls, but they delayed those until after they were set up for the night. Luis and Ted built a fire and started the grill. Before long the fresh Yucatan air was mingled with the aroma of burning charcoal and cooking. An hour later, their food was ready. After eating, they took turns showering before gathering around the campfire. Marcus led the group in some choruses on his guitar.

Before turning in, Ted gave a small Bible lesson and they had prayer. It had been a long day, and nobody in the group had to be forced to go to bed, especially knowing the next day they would be going into the jungle preserve that Luis had spoken about.

The next morning they had breakfast and broke camp before moving on. Their first stop of the day was Sian Ka'an which proved to be as awe inspiring as its reputation. Once again Luis proved himself to be a most informative guide, stopping often to reveal to them the exotic fauna and flora the Yucatan had to offer. Above their heads, hidden amongst the canopy, they could hear birds calling and howler monkeys stirring about. Occasionally one of the simians would cry out and it became all too plain the reason for their name.

As the group moved further into the interior, their exploration took on a higher level of intensity. Luis cautioned them to stay together. "Although the jungle is beautiful, it can also be deadly," he reminded them.

He slowed his steps, coming to a stop near a large tree. Cautioning the group to be silent, he pointed up so they could see a boa constrictor wrapped across a limb about seven feet above their heads. The limb of the tree crossed the trail and the snake looked big and fat and deadly. Kim, although naturally cautious, nonetheless, was fascinated with the sleeping reptile and wished to see it up close. The rest of the group backed away, led by Marcus. Only Kim, Ken, and Luis ventured closer to the deadly reptile as they inched their way toward it.

The snake's tail was wrapped along the tree's massive trunk. Kim's captivation with the snake grew as she marveled at its muscles, even in its relaxed state. The reptile's colors and markings seemed even more brilliant in the wild. She had seen several at the zoo in Columbus on a school trip, but in its natural habitat, the beast took on a reality she never thought possible.

"See the way the body looks fat?" Luis said. "He has eaten recently and now he is sleeping, gathering heat in the afternoon. Kim, come just a little closer."

Kim edged forward until she stood directly beneath the snake. On Luis' instructions, she carefully reached up with her hand and gently touched the body of the sleeping serpent, allowing her fingers to stroke the side. The scaly skin felt cold and rough to her touch, but in spite of that, she found the entire experience stimulating and exciting.

Luis reached gently and pulled her away. "They sometimes appear to be asleep, only to drop suddenly on some unsuspecting prey," he whispered, "and even though he looks well fed, that does not mean he will not attack if he feels threatened."

Following the brief excursion with the snake, Luis pointed to some markings along the base of a tree's trunk nearby. Deep parallel gashes had formed where the bark had been ripped away from the plant.

"Those look like the marks of a jaguar; maybe an ocelot, but definitely one of the big cats. We probably ought to move back toward the bus. We are still about ten miles from the campsite."

Returning to the bus, the group rode to the camp. Kim thought of the snake and the markings on the tree left behind by a large feline as she watched the trees and the fauna pass by. How many other dangers were out there? It was a world so different from Riverside, so different from anything she had ever experienced before. This world was wild and untamed. She wondered what else they would experience on this trip, and she knew that whatever it was, it would also be equally unexpected.

Arriving at the campsite, the group pitched their tents and started the campfire. Working together in teams, they took pride in their newly discovered skills. For most of them it was the first time they had ever camped out. The tents were modern, light-weight polyester structures with wide screened windows and broad entrances that

zipped shut to keep mosquitoes out. Each tent slept four to eight people, making it possible for the entire group to be accommodated by
using only four of them. Ted and Brenda slept in one tent, the girls in
another. Alfonso was teamed with Marcus, Terrell, Sean, and Ken, and
Pastor Jiménez with Rick, Jim, Raúl, and Juan. Like the previous night
they gathered around the fire after dinner and sang praise songs. When
it was time to retire for the night, the group settled quickly, anticipat-
ing the busy day ahead of them. They didn't know that they would have
a busy night as well.

*The jungle at night is noisy, but it becomes as still as a graveyard
whenever the great cat prowls. The jungle silences itself, the only natural defense against the deadly, stalking predator.*

*Stepping cautiously and silently along the tropical bed, not for
fear, but for hunting its prey, the cat smells a familiar odor. Like a
shark in deep waters, he senses its presence for miles, craving its salty
taste. The scent grows stronger as it nears the source.*

*The beast locates what it seeks, four structures similar to ones it
has seen before. There is also another odor intermingled with the one
it craves. A different odor; one that he has learned to fear! Now the big
cat's silence is both predatory and defensive in nature as he gingerly
lays his gigantic paws on the soft earth. Inching closer to the source,
the large cat's inner motor begins to purr involuntarily, a deep rumble
from inside its chest.*

*The structure rises before him. Both odors seep forth; simultane-
ously alluring and alarming him. Slowly he edges its nose through the
opening of the structure, and then his head. The cat's green eyes see
clearly in the dimness of the night and observes the source of the odor
lying on the earthen floor three feet in front of him.*

*He closes the distance between himself and his prey with speed
that defies imagination. The cat moves faster than should be possible
for an animal of his powerful size; a nocturnal blur faster than a blink.*

About to sink his teeth into his prey, he wonders why the bird hasn't fled; why it hasn't flinched or attempted to run for safety.

Suddenly the great cat is startled by a high piercing sound, quickly joined by another, and then another. He hears sounds coming from several directions at once and the odor that he has learned to fear permeates his nostrils. As quickly as he entered, the beast grabs his meal in his vise-like jaws, flees into the night, and escapes his enemy.

"What is it?" Luis hollered, flashing his light into the girl's tent.

Wendy, the first to scream, spoke up. "There was a cat in the tent."

The beam from Luis' flashlight illuminated the floor of the tent. There were feathers scattered about, with streaks of blood leading to an opening in the rear of the tent.

"This was no accident," Luis said, his fingers tracing the edge of the slit in the tent. "These feathers belong to an oscillated turkey, and it did not cut its way into the tent. It also did not gut itself or trail its blood in here."

He left the tent through the front opening. Rick, Jim, and Raúl followed closely behind. At the rear of the tent, the flashlights revealed more blood and feathers scattered about. Among the blood were several large footprints and a cigarette butt all too familiar to the boys. They were examining the butts when Pastor Jiménez interrupted them and sent them back to their tents.

"Okay, girls," he announced, "we are going to move you. You will have to sleep in the bus tonight. Luis, we will also have to set up a watch. I will go first and wake you at four. You might as well get some rest."

Luis saw the girls to the bus. "I will close the door, ladies, but the windows will have to remain open or you will not be able to stand the heat. I would suggest you put on a lot of insect repellant." Closing the door behind him, he went back to his cot where he laid down, knowing he would be awakened in the three hours ant it would be all the sleep he would get that night.

For a long time, Rick lay in his cot reflecting about what had happened. Listening to the nocturnal cadence of the jungle, he thought of how the cat came to be in the girl's tent. It didn't make any sense. He knew the source of the cigarettes butts, but what would León gain by harming the girls? Did he pick the wrong tent, thinking he was attacking the boys instead? What did it have to do with the box and the log? He felt a tinge of guilt, knowing that if anything had happened to Wendy or any of the other girls he wouldn't have been able to live with himself. Rick decided it was time to share the information with the entire group. It was time to tell them about the chest. Whatever the secret was, they needed to know, since now it appeared that they were all in danger. The problem would be how to inform everyone in privacy, which seemed impossible on this trip, but he had to think of a way before someone got hurt.

Before he fell asleep, an idea came to him.

Chapter Fourteen

The Mayans

The next morning Luis, thinking no one was paying attention, stepped behind the girl's tent once more to reexamine the tracks left by the cat. The early morning's light revealed the prints to be even larger than previously thought. After measuring the prints and assessing their size and stride, he shuddered, thinking how close the entire event could have ended in tragedy. Pastor Jiménez joined him, and the two men spoke in soft whispers.

Watching the two men from across the campsite, Rick knew instinctively the cat had been the big one; a jaguar. Even an ocelot, which is twice as large as the common house cat, would not have caused that much alarm. Rick silently thanked the Lord for protecting everyone.

During the night, before falling asleep, he figured out a way to communicate with the others by using the simple code that Ken and Kim taught them. He decided to try it out by leaving a message for Jim. Before leaving the tent he took a note pad from his backpack and wrote a simple note.

∨⊓⅃Γ⊡　⊃⊓Γ∨　⅃ᗧ⊐⊡

∨Γ⊃⊓　⅃ᐸ⅃⊡　⅃⊡⊐

Γ⅃ᐸ⅃.

He placed the note inside one of Jim's shoes and left the tent for breakfast. From his seat by the fire, he continued watching Luis and

Ted as they talked. They looked in Rick's direction, evidently deter-
mining there was no danger of Rick overhearing them as they stooped
beside the tracks left by the cat. Luis was measuring it by spreading
his fingers and laying his hand flat across the print. The expression on
Ted's face told Rick all he needed to know. Then Luis and Ted began
sliding their feet across the paw prints, erasing them. They followed
them until they were in the grass of the jungle and away from the
campsite.

Returning to the camp, Ted paused and looked at Rick. Rick wondered if they were somehow linking him to the attack, before realizing
that in some ways he was at fault. If this was about the chest then it
drove someone to follow them all the way into the jungles of Quintana
Roo. He was responsible for endangering the group. Realizing that
everyone was now involved in one way or another, he confirmed in his
mind the need for the Ten to help solve the mystery.

Twenty minutes later Jim woke, saw the note inside his shoe, studied it as he recalled the code, and shared the secret with Raúl and Juan.
That morning, while riding to Bacalar, all of the members of the Ten
were made aware of the chest and its contents. At first Wendy got angry at Rick and Jim, but then realized the boys had no way of knowing
the man would follow them into the jungle or do something so cruel
and dangerous. As far as they knew, the chest was just an old box.

They arrived at Bacalar just before noon, amazed at the development of the area. What Rick had envisioned as a simple cenote was in
reality an underground lake with the water a rich, deep blue.

"Why do they call it the Lake of Seven Colors?" he asked Luis.

Luis smiled, knowing once again that it would be Rick who would
ask the question first.

"It is because of the blue spectrum that changes at sunrise and
sunset. The cenote that we will visit is about three miles from here.
The water stays around eighty degrees, much warmer than the smaller
cenotes."

As promised, the cenote was one of the most beautiful sites they had ever seen. The water was incredibly clear and the group enjoyed diving and snorkeling for about three hours.

During a brief rest period, Rick overheard Luis, Ted, and Pastor Jiménez talking. He tried to appear as if he wasn't paying attention, although he saw Ted watching him suspiciously out of the corner of his eye.

"We should be safe enough tonight," Luis said.

"Are we sure that it was a real attack last night?" Ted asked.

Luis gave him a sober look. "The tent was not clawed open. If a jaguar had done it, the side of the tent would have been shredded instead of one clean slice. Also, the turkey did not enter the tent and kill itself. No, this was done to purposely draw a predator to the tent. Also, we found footprints that did not match anyone in the group, and since it rained yesterday morning, those prints had to have been made during the afternoon or later. But at least we will not have need to worry about anything tonight."

"Why is that?" Ted asked.

"Because the Mayans are very suspicious of strangers," Pastor Jiménez answered. "Even though they get a lot of tourists, they still remain a closed society. It took me almost four months to gain their confidence. If there are any strangers near the village other than us, they will know about it."

"Well, that's comforting," Ted said. He again stared at Rick but turned back to the pastor without saying anything to the Gideon Ten leader.

"How much progress *have* you made with the Mayans?" Ted asked Pastor Jiménez.

Pastor Jiménez smiled as he reflected on the ministry. "The Mayan people do not trust outsiders, including Mexicans. It took me several months before they trusted me. It took another two months before I had my first convert. We now have about sixty that attend our meetings, but if it were not for the Lord, we would not even be talking about this. I will not tell you how I came to get in with them but let us just say that no one will get near us tonight."

Rick had eavesdropped for as long as he dared without arousing Ted's suspicion. He grabbed his snorkel and headed back to the water, moving to the area of the lagoon where Raúl and Juan were standing with Jim.

"Okay, I just heard that the cat last night was definitely a jaguar."

"You mean *overheard* it," Jim said accusingly.

Rick chose to ignore the remark. "They also believe it wasn't an accident, because the tent was cut with a sharp object like a knife."

"The jaguar couldn't have done it?" Jim said.

"No, it would have slashed the tent. Also, they think the turkey was gutted and thrown into the tent."

"Then we are talking about attempted murder," Juan said, his face growing hard with the revelation. He looked back to where the ministers sat and realized from their expressions the information that Rick was sharing was the truth.

Rick nodded. "We need to let everyone know to be on the lookout."

Wendy swam to where the boys were. Mackenzie followed close behind.

"Are you talking about the attack last night?"

"Yes," said Rick. "We don't think it was an accident, and neither do the adults."

Mackenzie's eyes winced with fear. "Wait a minute," Mackenzie said. "Now I know where I saw him."

"Saw who?" Rick asked.

"At the ruins, there was a man that I thought looked familiar. He was one of the workers at the church."

Rick described León and Mackenzie agreed that was who it was.

"We must be getting close to something," Rick told the others, "if they feel threatened enough to follow us this far. Okay, this afternoon we'll let everyone know about the box and the log. We'll have to put our heads together on this one."

The others agreed and returned to swimming as Rick planned their next course of action.

The city of Bacalar holds one of the largest remaining populations of Mayans. The group was surprised to learn just how much the Mayan culture had influenced the lifestyles of Mexico and the Southwest United States. The Mayans were primarily a textile society, harvesting their own cotton, and making and blending their own dyes. Luis once again proved himself knowledgeable as a guide, leading them on a tour of the mills and the market places. His familiarity of the processes and customs was remarkable.

The Ten soon discovered the Mayans were a friendly and hard-working people, though they also discerned a degree of aloofness about them. The many pyramids the Mayans built were a testimonial to their architectural achievements, developed without sophisticated tools or measuring devices much like the Egyptian pyramids. The day was very pleasant and informative. That evening before the service, the group dined on traditional Mexican food.

Ted followed the preliminaries with the message. Working with a translator, who not only spoke in Spanish, but also used the Mayan dialect, Ted read from the Book of Acts, the seventeenth chapter and verse twenty-three.

For as I passed by, and beheld your devotions, I found an altar with this inscription, TO THE UNKNOWN GOD. Whom therefore ye ignorantly worship, him declare I unto you.

"Paul was a man who had traveled over much of the world and was educated in the greatest schools of his day."

Ted waited as his interpreter repeated the words he had spoken before continuing.

"Paul was born with the name Saul and he came from a great city like yours named Tarsus. He was very dedicated to his religion and persecuted many of his people because they began believing in a different God than the one he believed. This is similar to the way some of your own people have treated you since you have come to worship Jesus.

"Saul was blinded while on his way to Damascus by a great light that appeared from above. In the midst of the light came a voice. It was the voice of Jesus, the very God that he fought against. He accepted Jesus as his Lord and was healed of his blindness. Then he changed his name to Paul and began telling everyone about this great God named Jesus.

"His enthusiasm took him over a great sea into lands where he had many adventures and met many people. His journey led him to a large city named Athens. One day while he was walking through their great market place, he noticed an altar dedicated to the unknown god.

"Later that day he met some wise men of the city who challenged his beliefs until Paul reminded them of their unknown god. In all of their studies and searching for knowledge, they found they still did not have the answers to all of their questions. But Paul told them that he knew who the unknown god was.

"In times past, you as Mayans have worshipped many gods. The great plumed serpent Kukulkán is still feared by your people today. But he is a god that destroys and offers nothing but pain and death. I am speaking today about a God who gives life.

"You have a god for fire, wind, rain, and the sun, but in your beliefs, they only control those specific elements. I am speaking of a God so great, that he created those things simply by speaking them into existence. Before he spoke there was nothing; no sun, no moon, no air. He is the only true God, and as such, the only one that should be worshipped.

"I stand here today, just like Paul did that day in Athens, to declare to you that the unknown and true God is Jesus. By His Word He spoke and created the world and the stars, and by the same Word, He can speak happiness and contentment into your lives.

"Many of you have already discovered this joy that I am offering, but to those of you who haven't, the opportunity to meet and experience this wonderful God as your Lord and Savior is available to you right here, right now."

Pastor Jiménez was pleased to see four new people come forward to accept Christ. The trip had been a success and the visitors from the states had been more than a blessing to his church and to the Mayans. They did not just come to buy wares, like many of the other tourists, but they came to share and to give. Still, it bothered him about the attack. He felt someone in the group knew at least a small part about what had happened and why it may have happened. If he were a betting man, he would have put his money on Rick or Jim. Probably Rick, as Jim seemed to be more of a follower. For whatever reason, Rick had not decided to confide in him or Ted. Maybe he would later. Pastor Jiménez just hoped nobody would not get hurt or killed before that happened.

Chapter Fifteen

Ted's Warning

The Ten's trek through the Yucatan ended a day later as an exhausted but excited group pulled up in front of the church with a dozen people or so waiting to take the weary campers home. *Señor* and *señora* Galante were there to gather Raúl, Jim, Rick, and Alfonso.

Before leaving with her host family, Wendy pulled Rick aside, walking him into the vestibule of the church. She looked around carefully to make sure they were alone. Seeing no one, she leaned close to him and began whispering.

"Rick," she began, "I just want to say that Mackenzie and I are more than willing to help you guys figure out what to do. It appears as if you've uncovered another adventure. I just wish it didn't always involve danger."

Rick was surprised to see just how tired she looked, and he couldn't recall ever seeing her when her auburn hair wasn't flawlessly combed, but being a wiser man than before, he didn't say anything.

"Wendy, I never thought that these men would do something so extreme that they would try and kill someone. I would never have placed you in danger on purpose."

"I know that. It was just the Lord that saved us, because when I woke and saw that jaguar, I almost froze. If I hadn't screamed that big cat would have probably killed me and the rest of the girls before leaving. As scary as the whole thing was, I want you to know I don't blame you and neither do the other girls. As far as what to do with the chest, we want to help you, because we know that you'll do the right thing in the end."

Rick appreciated her sincerity, but still couldn't help feeling guilty.

He gave her an engaging smile in spite of the empty feeling he had inside. He wondered how he could have ever doubted her where Juan was concerned. How do you question someone that you care for about feelings that are based on suspicions? He had had a crush on Wendy ever since the second grade, only to find out that she cared for him too but had been waiting for him to make the first move. He knew she wouldn't throw away eight years for nothing, and there probably wasn't anything between her and Juan. He almost let the whole thing drop, but in typical *Rick fashion*, he ignored any warnings and asked the question anyway.

"Wendy, about when we arrived here. You and Juan…?"

"I know," she said blushing. "And I'm sorry. The truth is I started hanging around him because I wanted to make you mad. After all, you chose a baseball trivia game over me."

Rick drew in an unsuspected gulp of air. "How did you know about that?"

"I just found out. That's not important," she said, dismissing the statement. "Anyway, about Juan, it was only after I began talking to him that I found him to be interesting, and not too different from most teenagers from the states. He needs a friend, and I'm glad to see that he began opening up to you and Jim on the trip. Do you know he's a champion boxer?"

Rick nodded. He could still feel the jabs to the face, the punch to the gut, and most of all, the uppercut knockout punch. But what troubled him the most about the information was that Wendy had purposely tried and succeeded at making him jealous. Why would she even do such a thing? Was she testing him to find out how much he really cared for her? Didn't she know he had been smitten with her from the moment he first laid eyes on her?

Rick lost himself in thought, wondering about Wendy's deception, or was it really a deception? Could she have really been attracted to the older teen? Could it have been on a subconscious level? Maybe he needed to talk to Ken about it. Rick knew Juan was handsome, athletic, and probably more experienced with girls than he was. His thoughts were interrupted by Wendy's next statement.

"He tries so hard to make his father proud of him," Wendy said, revealing a side of Juan that Rick had never imagined, "but instead his father pays more attention to other boxers who he's trying to win to the Lord." Wendy seeing that her host family was waiting, added, "It's sad in a way, and I don't know the answer, but I know that you usually find a way to break down those kinds of barriers. I have to be going but let Mackenzie and myself know when we're getting together as a group."

He watched as she ran to catch her ride. After she was gone, Juan entered the small lobby and approached Rick.

"Rick, can we talk?"

Rick looked at the Galantes and saw they hadn't loaded their SUV yet. "I have a few minutes."

Juan looked about to assure that he and Rick were alone.

"I know you have to meet with the rest of the group because of this chest. With you and Jim staying with Raúl in Maxcanú, it will make it difficult to get everyone together, so I talked with my father and I am bringing the rest of the group to the Galante's tomorrow for a pool party. We will be there around eleven."

"Thanks, Juan. That will be a huge help." As an afterthought Rick added, "I want you to stay for the meeting also, if you don't mind."

The pastor's son beamed with pride. "Thank you. I would consider it an honor."

As Juan was leaving, Ted entered the church and grabbed Rick roughly by the elbow. "We need to talk," he said. From the force of the hold he had on Rick's arm, Rick knew it wasn't going to be a pleasant conversation.

Rick felt his throat constrict and breathing became difficult. Ted hadn't given him a request; it had been a statement of intent. Looking for help he caught one last glimpse of Juan as he walked outside. He turned back to face an upset Ted who was glaring at him.

"Rick, I don't know what you are up to, but I believe you know more about what's happening than you're telling. I know the attack at Sian Ka'an was no accident and for the rest of the trip I saw you kids passing notes with funny symbols. Don't think it fooled me. I can break your code if I have to. Now, what's going on?"

Rick knew it was time to come clean, but the only facts he had were in a box, and they were four hundred years old. Other than that, they had only speculations and suspicions, and neither were enough with which to take action.

Rick took a deep breath. "Ted, it all started the first day we worked on the foundation. When the pastor called it for the day, our ride hadn't arrived yet, so we decided to work a little longer. After about ten minutes or so we decided it was getting too hot so we decided to quit. As we were leaving the foundation to put our tools away, I saw something shiny sticking out of the ground. After digging all around it, we pulled out a small chest. We took it home and opened it up. Inside the chest were a dagger, some Spanish doubloons, and a ship's log.

"The log was from a ship called the Ocean Shark. Jim and I, with the help of Raúl have discovered the log possibly belonged to a former mayor of Mérida and Governor of the Yucatan. It's also possible that it was the same governor who donated the land to the Catholic Church for a mission. That's all that we know, except we think the same person that set up the attack at the reservation also broke into the bunkhouse and was searching for the box."

"And what do you base that on?" Ted asked, his opinion of Rick's guilt abating by the second.

"Because of the footprints outside the bunkhouse window," Rick answered. "They were the same as the ones in the jungle. Even the cigarette butt was the same brand, and even though we don't know for sure who they belong to, we think it was León."

Rick found it difficult to read Ted's reaction as his face had become hardened with a blend of anger, disgust, confusion, and disappointment, making it difficult for Rick to determine which emotion was directed at him and which to Léon.

"The day worker?" Ted asked.

Rick nodded.

Ted considered what Rick said. "Pastor Jiménez told me that León and Rocky have not shown up for work since the group left for the interior. Even if it is true that León was responsible for the jaguar incident, we still don't have enough evidence to call the police.

"Look, Rick, I know you could never have anticipated the jaguar attack in the jungle. No one could, because if the box is what they want, how would killing someone have gotten it back? The only reason I can think of is the attack was a warning for you to back off. Whether or not the box and its contents are recovered, whoever was behind the attack at Sian Ka'an wants you boys to stop searching for answers."

In spite of himself, Ted started to laugh and his blue eyes sparkled. The reaction took Rick by surprise until Ted said, "Rick, how is it you keep getting into so much trouble, when all you're really trying to do is the right thing?"

Relief swept over Rick like a springtime rain, a contrast from the tension he had sensed just a moment before. "It's a gift. I'm just talented that way I guess."

Ted shook his head in disbelief. "Well, it's time for you to leave. We still have five more days to spend down here. I would suggest that you bring the box with you the next time you come into town and turn it over to the pastor or myself so we can decide what to do with it. Also, try and stay out of trouble, okay? And, Rick, watch your back. They might still be gunning for you guys. Meanwhile I'll discuss this with Pastor Jiménez."

"Thanks, Ted. We'll let you know if we find out anything or if anything else suspicious happens."

As he rode home, his thoughts were on the next day's meeting. The group had always come through in the past. He hoped they would do so again. He knew he couldn't do it by himself, or with just Jim and Raúl's help. The Ten would find the answers, he was sure of it. They had never let him down before.

Chapter Sixteen

Abduction

The next morning, Juan arrived with the group at eleven o'clock. *Señora* Galante served them ham and turkey sandwiches for lunch, after which the group played in the pool for about three hours. When the Yucatan sun became too hot, they all retreated to the safety of the bunkhouse. Raúl brought the box out of its hiding place and shared the contents with the rest of the group.

Opening the box, Raúl pulled out the journal, the dagger, and the doubloons. As he took out the dagger, the girls marveled at the beauty of the weapon's handle. They turned it over to allow the afternoon sun to reflect off the jewels and sent tiny, pixie-like lights all throughout the bunkhouse. They passed the dagger around as Raúl shared with them the doubloons and the logbook. Ken, who was able to read Spanish, took the journal and began thumbing through it.

Wendy and Mackenzie lay down on the hammocks for a siesta and soon dozed off as the heat built up from the rising temperature. The others drifted away from the hammocks, allowing them to get their rest. As the room got quieter, Rick and Juan reexamined the knife, entranced by the way the blood had stained the edge dark red in places, like a crimson highlight along the side of the silvery surface.

Kim and Raúl looked over Ken's shoulder as he thumbed his way through the old journal. Ken bunched his eyebrows and stuck out his tongue out of the corner of his mouth as he concentrated on the ancient log. It was his usual pose whenever he got lost in a new project. Rising from his chair, he crossed the room and held the book up to the window, allowing the bright, afternoon sunlight to shine directly on it.

Ken pointed to some pages in the log for January. "Did you notice this?" he said. "It's different from the handwriting in May. See the long looping letters whenever he makes an el? Also, his T's are crossed very sharply, and the I's are prominently dotted. Now look at the change after May. The writing is weaker, the T's are barely crossed, and he shows poor attention to detail. Not only that, but the writer is now left-handed."

Raúl's face contorted in confusion. He had never thought of the difference in writing. "What are you talking about?"

Rick saw Raúl's frustration and wondered what it was like to talk to Ken in a second language when most people found it difficult to follow him with English as their mother tongue.

Before he could explain, Kim laughingly said, "Ken studied hand-writing analysis last year. Now he's always looking for an opportunity to use it."

Ken rolled his eyes and ignored his sister. "I prefer the term gra-phology. The other term sounds like something you would see at a carnival side show." Kim rolled her eyes in response to his rebuttal. Ken continued. "There is something definitely different about the two entrees though. Let me show you."

He pointed to the writing on one of the pages in December.

"Look at the peculiar slant of the letters here. A left-handed per-son turns his hand in order to write his letters from left to right with an upward slant, the way we were taught in school."

The others looked at the journal and realized what Ken was talking about. Raúl couldn't believe he hadn't noticed it before.

"Also, there's the difference in the detail of the writing. Look here at the way he crosses his T's; they're always precise. That indicates a perfectionist, or at least someone who pays careful attention to the details of proper writing. This person had a degree of education and culture, but here, he misses occasionally. And look at the I's. Here, they are always dotted, but in May they get missed, or they're off cen-ter. This is indicative of a disorganized person. Even the E's; in the earlier entrees they are open, revealing confidence, while here they are closed, which usually means a very secretive, insecure person, possibly even on the verge of paranoia.

"The last clue is the broken style in the early writings. This is the writing style of a very intuitive individual, but not here. This person is full of suspicion and maybe even envy. It's definitely not the same person writing."

By this time, Rick, having overheard Ken talking about the handwriting, left Juan and Jim and joined the discussion.

"So, what's your take on all that?" he asked.

Ken hesitated briefly. "I'm not sure how to explain this, because this is even wilder than a ship's captain and pirate becoming a governor."

He turned to a passage later in the log that indicated the Captain wore his sword on his right side. "The only reason someone wears a sword on his right side is because he's left-handed. It would be too awkward to draw it out of its sheath if he wore it on the left. Even if he drew it with the right hand, the split second it would take to switch it over to the left hand would have meant the difference between life and death.

"If what I'm thinking is true, then Captain Enrique Blood was not the Governor of the Yucatan, alias or otherwise. Captain Blood never made it out of Superstition Cove."

Ken stopped talking to allow what he said to sink in. Kim's mouth flew open in surprise and the others looked back and forth, registering each other's expressions. It soon became evident to the others that they had not even considered the possibility.

"I might even be able to prove it," Ken continued, "if I can get to a library that has some historical records. I think the man who became the Governor of Yucatan was the first mate Sanchez. The log implies that Blood killed everyone, but what if he lost that fight with his first mate? What if Sanchez took on the identity of Captain Blood? That would account for the lack of confidence in the latter part of the log.

Captain Blood was a man of sophistication. He was a leader, while Sanchez was an insurrectionist, a rebel, a mutineer"

The silence was crushing. Rick was especially surprised as he had no idea the new adventure had historical ramifications. If Ken was right, the first mate would have risen in politics with the wealth gained from *the terra firma flota*, but he wouldn't have had sufficient leadership qualities to hold it all together, much less the social graces or knowledge of governmental procedures to be an effective politician.

"Would it have made much difference who was the Governor?" Rick asked. "How would that have changed anything?"

Ken smiled, his eyes twinkling the way they always did when he was learning something new. His theory, if true, would be even more radical than a pirate captain taking a political office.

"The difference is how the treasure would have been handled. Blood would have built an empire with it. He was disciplined and in control. Sanchez would have burned through it like kindling until he eventually was left with nothing, and I think that's what happened. That's why he started selling everything off; because he was going broke. Also, there would have been the matter of hiding the treasure. Blood would have never hid it in something as volatile as a cenote. I'm almost positive the man that finished that log was Sanchez, and he hid this logbook along with the dagger and the doubloons. I think I know why he did it and, even though I don't have the evidence just now, I think I can prove it."

Rick thought about Ken's theory. The only answer would be to return to the Historical Museum and let Ken and Raúl look through the archives together. That was where the answers would be found, he was sure of it. He was also sure that his friends would find it, but would finding the answer help them know the reason for the attack? And, would they be safe until then? Was the jaguar attack a solitary event, or would there be other incidents?

They made plans to go into Mérida in two days. Juan and Ken were to meet Jim, Rick, and Raúl to finish the research. Rick, however, wondered if the discovery of treasure would lead to the end of their adventure or another potential tragedy.

Thursday morning at nine o'clock sharp, Raúl, Jim, and Rick stood in front of the Historical Museum of the Yucatan waiting for the others. Ten minutes later, Juan pulled up in the church's van, with Ken, Kim, and Monica. Rick took note that Monica was sitting in the front seat next to Juan. He smiled at the image and wondered to himself if Monica would be sitting there if Wendy had come along, but he didn't worry about it as he believed that he and Juan had settled their differences during the trip.

The library portion of the museum was practically empty, but then, it probably stayed that way most of the time during the week, thought Rick. Raúl went to the section that held all the land records that he had visited several weeks before and pulled down a volume. He carried it to a study desk and set it down. When he opened the records to 1604, Ken immediately began scanning the entrees for the name Cortez. There were several recordings in May of that year, mostly land purchases.

"Did you notice these land deals?" Ken asked.

"Yes," Raúl answered, "but we weren't concentrating on them at the time."

"I need to see the land transactions for the last five months of 1604. I have a hunch."

When Raúl went back to the shelves to pull down the next volume, he found them to be out of sequence. The remaining journals were in order, but the journal for the end of the year 1604 was missing. Raúl checked through the next twenty volumes but could not locate the one he was searching for.

After telling Ken, the boys approached the librarian's desk together. Ken began speaking in his best Spanish, asking if she knew where the missing volume was. Raúl took over by translating for Ken. Before that, Ken had told the confused woman that he was the United States and he had a journal with his name missing.

The librarian swept wispy brown hair from her face. "It seems to me," she said with a thin voice, "that there was someone else looking over those very same records about two months ago." She closed her dark brown eyes as she concentrated on the man's name. Unable to come up with it, she added, "I believe he said that he was a graduate student from the states, but I can't recall his name"

Eavesdropping on the conversation, Rick picked up on the few words he understood. "Ask her if the man's name was Rocky," he said.

At the mention of the name, the woman got excited and began nodding her head vigorously. She told of the red-headed American who searched the records for several days. He said that he was researching for a thesis on the historical land development of the Yucatan.

The group huddled around the table again and opened the journals, wondering what they should do next. Ken soon found himself lost in the search once more, bouncing ideas off Kim and Raúl. Even though the ledgers were not in sequence, he found obscure references to additional purchases by Enrique Cortez. Ken asked Raúl if he knew where they could view any laws or edicts the Governor would have signed into effect during his tenure as Mayor or Governor.

"I want to compare his signatures with what I've seen so far."

Raúl suggested they ask the librarian again and he and Ken returned to the reference desk with Kim in tow. She directed them to some reference books that may have some copies of documents signed by the governor. As the others studied the records, Rick, with Juan and Jim decided to take a stroll through the rest of the museum.

An hour later, the three boys were about to return to the research center, hoping that Ken was finished looking through the ancient tomes, when Jim excused himself to go to the restroom. Rick and Juan decided to wait for him by the stairs. They stood talking about the jaguar attack when Rick felt something sharp pressed into his back. He started to turn but a hand grabbed his shoulder and pulled him backwards. An arm was wrapped around his neck, choking off his oxygen and the point in his back became more pronounced.

"Hello, Ricky," Rocky said, his voice a menacing whisper.

Rick felt himself blacking out, but before he passed out he saw León position himself behind Juan. The huge Mexican wore a cruel look of scorn on his face.

Juan turned to face the day laborer, but León held a gun on the older teen. He smiled and said, "I'd like to take you on, kid, but it would make too much of a fuss."

Jim came out of the restroom just as Rocky laid the limp body of Rick onto the library's marble floor. He vacillated as the *fight or flight* response battled for control of his mind and body. Before he could decide, Rocky said, "Don't even think about it. I have a knife, and one false step and I'll cut your buddy to ribbons and disappear before you can return. Now get over here and help pick up your friend. Drag him out to the car. Either one of you tries anything funny, and León will shoot both of you. Now let's go."

Jim put his arms underneath Rick's and hoisted him upwards. He pulled Rick across the foyer, dragging Rick's heels along the floor, and out the door where Rocky's car was parked at the curb with its engine still idling. The two adults shoved the boys into the back, taking the time to tie their hands first. The car peeled out, squealing tires and leaving the smell of burnt rubber as it sped away.

At the top of the stairs, Kim watched as the car disappeared around the corner. Shaking with fear, she rushed back to the others, a jumbled knot of thoughts passing through her head. *What kind of a car were they in? How many men were there? Could there have been another man waiting in the car? Did they have one or two guns? Where were they going?*

She was too late to prevent them from being kidnapped, but she wasn't too late to get help. She burst into the room where Ken and Raúl were going over the logs and screamed, "They've kidnapped the guys. Call the police."

Chapter Seventeen
A Watery Grave

Rick regained consciousness as the car jostled him awake, only to find his hands tied with rope. He tried maneuvering his body to a more upright position, but found he was crammed in the middle of Rocky's backseat between Jim and Juan. His head hurt from where he had been choked unconscious, reminding him of the forty seconds he lasted in the ring with Juan. Other than that, he realized he hadn't been harmed yet. He struggled with his bonds, twisting them back and forth, but found them too tight to escape from. Rocky turned in the front seat and looked at his captives with a menacing smile. He waved the gun at the boys even though he knew that in their current condition they could offer little or no resistance. Looking into the man's eyes, Rick became aware of the men's true intentions. He and his two friends were not coming back from this drive.

Rick was surprised to find they were traveling in an eastward direction from the city. If their intention was to force them to tell where the treasure was, they were going in the wrong direction. The area called Superstition Cove was to the west. Something was seriously wrong.

"You know, the treasure isn't this direction," Rick said, hoping to keep the fear out of his voice. "It's back in Maxcanú. We can take you to it, but you'll have to drive us there."

Rocky let out a cold laugh. His eyes taunted as he glared at them. "Ricky, never try to kid a kidder. First of all, you don't know where it is, and secondly, we don't need the chest, and we definitely don't need any advice from you. In a way, I'm glad you have the box, because it won't tell you anything we don't already know, and the fact that you've hidden it again means no one else will learn anything from it. Meanwhile, you're going to another of the good captain's possessions; a little tract of land, untouched by the developers. It'll be at least ten years before they'll find your bodies, if at all."

Rocky's menacing smile confirmed Rick's fears. He and his two friends were destined to disappear for no other reason than to give Rocky and León time to get out of the country. While the authorities searched in vain for the two guests from the United States and a pastor's son, the two pirates would escape undetected. They could always return at a later date and complete their search.

"We have it all set," Rocky said. "My only problem is *you* right now. I already know you've been checking out the museums. I also know you've taken some daytrips out near the coast."

Rocky's grin grew even larger and crueler when he saw Rick's reaction. Rick wondered if Rocky knew everything that the group did about Captain Blood. Did they know about their suspicion concerning the real writer of the logs was the Ocean Shark's first mate, Sanchez?

"That other kid that led you there may even be convincing enough to lead the police back to the coast," Rocky said with a laugh that bordered on malice, "but he won't find you there."

Rick wondered what Rocky was talking about. The log stated that the treasure was in the fourth cenote near the edge of the jungle, but that was in the opposite direction. What were these two men doing taking them east? He saw a sign pointing to Motul. León turned northeast toward Dzidzantún.

"We searched almost all of the land that Governor Cortez owned," Rocky said. "In fact, to make sure no one else found it by mistake, I took several volumes from the library. I came down here to study the colonization of the Yucatan for my thesis at the University of Houston. While studying the records, I came across the name Don Cortez, the Governor who literally appeared out of nowhere. Then I saw the records of all the purchases and I asked myself, 'Where did all the money come from?'"

Rick's eyes met Jim's. Jim turned his head and stared straight ahead, showing no emotion. Rick wondered if he had even heard Rocky talking or if he was in shock. Rick turned his head and looked at Juan. The older boy was slumped over, his head resting against the window. There was a knot on the side of his head where León had struck him with his revolver before shoving him into the car.

"That's really interesting, Rocky, but does that justify assault and kidnapping. I'm pretty sure those offenses are against the law in Mexico as well the United States."

Rocky laughed again, acting as if he hadn't even heard Rick, and continued talking, boasting of his supposed success. "That was when I became suspicious. Then I thought to myself, where did he get all his wealth? Knowing how piracy was so rampant in the Caribbean, I put two and two together and figured he had his treasure hidden somewhere in the Yucatan.

"Funny thing though, I was never able to determine where it was. However, I found out that museums have more information than they realize. They possessed the daily journals of Governor Enrique Cortez, but no one put the significance of the writings together until I came along. And then, just as I'm closing in on a major discovery, you kids come along and find a box with the ship's log in it."

Rick made a short gasp as León drove the car over a deep rut. Trying not to react to the news, he couldn't help but reveal his reaction upon hearing Rocky mention the ship's log. *So, Rocky knew what was in the chest.*

"That's right. I knew what you dug up that first day. That was my entire purpose of being on that construction crew. I believed it was buried somewhere on that property. When you kids found it, I thought everything was over, but then I realized that I had more pieces to the puzzle than you did."

Rick gave a wry smile, in spite of his circumstances. He knew the real secret of Superstition Cove and Rocky didn't. He knew for certain the source of the ship's wealth, and he was pretty sure that a first mate named Sanchez had murdered the captain of the Ocean Shark. Rocky's thesis could have launched him into international fame, but now he was chasing after a treasure that he would probably never find.

"Your group would have been gone in another week. The only problem is I didn't know who you told about the chest. Did you know that Cortez even mentions the log in his political diaries? The man must have been an idiot. Man, I've checked almost a million square acres with metal detectors. I found nothing, but I did make some connections for smuggling Mayan artifacts out of the country. It pays more than an associate professorship at a university, that's for sure. What I became afraid of was that somehow you and the others would discover my side business, since it coincides with areas that you would possibly be visiting while looking for the treasure. We tried scaring you away with the jaguar. It should have worked, too, but the one girl screamed and scared the cat away. If someone had been seriously hurt or even killed, your group would have packed up immediately and left, but that didn't happen. Anyway, since you would have been gone in a couple of weeks, I planned to return, finish my search, and still make a fortune as a smuggler."

León steered the car off the main road onto a two-lane dirt path. Rick knew that each minute that passed would take them even further from civilization and any possibility of being rescued.

The sun was setting low in the sky and Rocky had evidently gotten tired of talking. Any other time that would have been a relief, but Rick would have given almost anything for some noise to take his mind off their present predicament. The road that had changed from asphalt to dirt now appeared to be nothing more than tire tracks crushing through the overgrown grass and shrubs.

Rick felt a small, sharp nick on the side of the seat belt lying across his lap. It wasn't much, but it was better than nothing. Forcing the rope across the nick over and over, he worked at cutting his bonds, though it seemed as doable as bailing out the ocean.

The air was tepid in the hold of the Spanish Corsair. Above the mizzen-mast flew the Jolly Roger, the flag recognized by pirates and sailors everywhere. The black banner rippled in the breeze, proudly waving at the sun and standing defiantly against the wind, the clouds, any other ships, and the British Empire. Rick the Barber, the notorious defender of the Barbary Coast examined his shackles. The scourge of the ocean, Rocky the sea dog, his nemesis, had captured him and placed him in irons. The rats in the hole scurried about, but for the most part left him alone. Rick knew he was still too healthy for them to fool with, but he also knew that he had to get out of the shackles before it was too late.

The Barber saw the condition of the irons that had him tethered to the ship's hull. The sea air had rusted the hinges of the ring that held his chains. He worked them back and forth, back and forth. The brave captain did not fear being overheard. He had fought the cowardly pirate many times off the coast of Florida, Cuba, The Bahamas, Haiti, and Bermuda, and had beaten him back every time. If he could get loose from his chains he would grab a cutlass and give the scurvy dog a thrashing he would not soon forget.

He worked the rusty hinge plate, forcing it back and forth, over and over, each creak louder than the previous one until finally the cacophonous uproar climaxed in one huge explosion.

"Get out," Rocky said, pulling the passenger-side, rear door open. He reached inside and yanked a semi-conscious Jim out of the car. Rick's bonds were loose, but even though he knew he could probably free himself, he was no match against two grown men armed with a knife and a gun.

León wrenched Juan out from the other side, the teenager reeling unsteadily on his feet. Juan was awake now, but the wound on the side of his head where León hit him was still seeping blood. The car was parked in a shallow clearing near the edge of a small jungle. The two men shoved the boys toward the tree line, the gun still leveled on them.

Rick knew they were walking to their execution. A nauseated feeling crept into his stomach and he could feel bile forming in his throat. Jim was paler than usual, and Juan was still silent and wobbly, but a look of defiance still emanated from his eyes. Rick felt he was only biding his time before he would make his move, but Rick knew there would be no way he could do anything against the two men in his current condition, even with all of his boxing skills.

"You know, Ricky boy," Rocky said, "You and your group had me worried. The jaguar may not have worked, but this will."

Rick choked back a reply. He hated when Rocky called him Ricky boy, but Jim was growing visibly weaker by the second and Juan was two degrees shy of being comatose. Rick knew he couldn't expect help from either of them.

Juan in his drunken-like state finally had enough consciousness to spin on León, but the larger man anticipated the move and drove a meaty fist into the boy's stomach. Juan doubled over in pain, the wind completely knocked out of him. As he gasped for oxygen, León smashed him in the face, knocking him down.

As the teen lay on the ground, León dragged him the last twenty feet and dropped him down a hole. Rick heard the splash, but in his state of shock, he hadn't taken the time to count the seconds. He knew the drop probably killed Juan, and even if it didn't, there was no telling how deep the grotto was. An injured person couldn't tread water very long, and especially one with his hands tied behind his back. He wouldn't be able to tread at all.

Rick, imagining the worst, pulled his arms free and ran toward the hole. His movement was so fast that he was past León before the man realized what was happening. Not even stopping long enough take a deep breath, as he plunged into the darkness. As he fell he screamed out, "Murderer."

Rick tucked his head in, pulled his legs up, and drew a quick breath as he slammed into the inky pool. The water grabbed him like a giant talon, crushing the breath out of him. Even though he knew the water would be cold, he was totally unprepared for the frigidness that engulfed him. This was not a warm pool like the cenote they had visited in Bacalar. Rick kicked for the surface, discarding the rest of the rope that still clung to his wrists. As he broke the surface, he gasped desperately for air, filling his lungs with the freezing oxygen. The frigid conditions stimulated him and he immediately realized the precarious position he was in. He took another deep breath and dove beneath the surface. Rick flung his arms around, frantically trying to find Juan as the water entombed him like a wet coffin. He resurfaced and was about to dive again when he felt something brush against his foot. He dove once more beneath the murky water and grabbed Juan, pulling the larger boy up by putting his arm underneath Juan's chin and kicking for the surface.

Just as his head popped out of the water, Rick heard another splash, and knew it was Jim. He wondered if his best friend was unconscious as well. Rick knew he couldn't save them both. He only had a split second to decide, though he prayed in his heart that God wouldn't force him to choose. In the dim light that remained inside the cavern Rick saw a small strip of land along the cave's wall. He began stroking, kicking hard toward the shore. Behind him he heard Jim burst forth out of the water. Knowing his friend was still alive encouraged him. Reaching the small beach, he lifted Juan out of the water before diving back in to help Jim.

With each stroke, Rick contemplated their situation. No one knew where they were, and there was no way to get out of the cave. Even if all three of them survived the night, they would either slowly starve to death or die of hypothermia. As he stroked his way toward Jim, Rick wrestled with the knowledge that he had just caused the death of himself and two others. They needed a miracle.

Chapter Eighteen

Ken's Discovery

Kim burst into the research library on the verge of hysteria, much to the distress of the librarian. It was several minutes before the others could calm her down enough to understand what she was talking about. When she finally got the story out, Ken attempted to get as much information from her as possible while the librarian called the police.

"Did you happen to see what kind of a car it was?" Ken asked.

"I don't know...a blue one. They all look alike. It was dark blue."

"León drives a bark blue Ford," Ken said. "I've seen him drive it to work." He turned to Raúl. "Have the librarian tell the police to be on the lookout for a dark blue Ford Taurus. I don't know what year, but it looks to be several years old."

After Raúl left, Ken sat down and began studying the ledgers again.

"WHAT ARE YOU DOING? THIS STUFF DOESN'T MATTER NOW," screamed Kim. Several patrons looked her way, knowing something was happening, but no one said anything to the girl from the States.

Ken removed his glasses and pinched his nose. After closing his eyes for a few seconds, he replaced his glasses and continued to scan the documents anyway. "I have to finish this in order to know where they took the guys. I only have two more journals to go through."

Kim looked at her brother strangely, partially wondering if he had lost his mind and was reacting to her news in a state of shock, but knowing Ken, she knew he had a plan and was working it the best he knew how. In a calmer voice, she asked, "What will that tell you?"

"Look, I need your help," he answered. "Rocky must have hidden some of the ledgers because they held information about land purchases that were recorded between July of 1604 and March of 1605. Sanchez continued to purchase land for several years, but then began selling off his land after he became Governor. Some of the land, however, was purchased by Captain Blood before Sanchez killed him.

"Look here," he said, showing a sale in 1611, and another in 1612. "I've looked through some of his historical records, and I'm convinced that Sanchez was slowly going insane. Maybe it was from the pressure of hiding his past, but I think there was something else going on instead. I think he lost his fortune and I think I know how, but right now we have to locate some holdings that he hadn't given away or sold and that we don't have records for. It's those areas that Rocky will more than likely go to either hide out for a while or to get rid of the boys. Because we don't have all the records, we'll have to pray that the property we need is in the early journals. The plot of land we want will probably be in an area that's undeveloped even today."

Kim finally understood what her brother was searching for and began examining one of the journals. By the time the police and Pastor Jiménez arrived, they had narrowed it down to three possible locations. All Ken had to do was convince the police that he knew what he was talking about.

The detective in charge of the investigation was Lieutenant Hector Gonzalez, a short, pasty looking man with a dark mustache that contrasted sharply with his graying hair. His dark eyes were sunk deeply into a fleshy face, resulting in an even greater emphasis of his portly physique. He listened to Kim's description of the abduction, holding an anxious Ken at bay with his upheld hand.

"And you say you saw at least one gun and a knife?" he asked as he scribbled notes on a pad.

Kim's eyes were still red from crying. She thought she couldn't cry anymore until she recalled the weapons. She feared for Rick and Jim, who she had known most of her life, and also for Juan, who she had known only a few weeks. Ted had been contacted and Kim knew the first person he would have advised would have been Pastor Jiménez. True to her suspicion, the two ministers arrived together as she was talking to the detective.

"Who is in charge here?" the pastor said. The desperation on his face was immediately apparent. "I am the pastor of *la Iglesia de Cristo el Rey* and my son is one of the kidnapped boys."

Detective Gonzalez made a motion with his hand intended to calm the minister and offered the pastor a seat beside him.

"I know of your church, pastor Jiménez. It is a great work in the city."

He finished with Kim and dismissed her before turning back to the pastor. "Pastor Jiménez, I have officers all over the Yucatan looking for the car. I have all confidence that they will be found within the hour."

Ted gave Pastor Jiménez a look that said he was doubtful they could solve it that fast.

Kim was finally able to get the detective to listen to Ken's idea by forcing her way into the conversation.

"My brother has some possible locations if you have time to listen."

Detective Gonzalez's face flushed with irritation, but he stopped talking and allowed Ken to speak.

"I've narrowed it down to three specific locations," Ken said, taking control of the meeting. "One is south of here, one is west, and the last one is to the east."

"And how did you come to these conclusions?" Lt. Gonzalez asked.

Ken explained about the ledgers and his efforts to compare them to land sales later. "We have records of early purchases, but there are no records of sales. I can't fully explain it right now, but the land purchases were done by one man, and the man who sold the properties wasn't aware of those tracts of land."

Gonzalez scrunched his face, looking at the ledgers like they were diseased or something.

"Couldn't there possibly be more than just three? Isn't it possible that we do not even know about one or two of the properties that this Rocky might know of?"

"It's possible sir, but do you have any ideas that are any better? At least this isn't shooting in the dark."

Gonzalez thought hard about his prospects. He would never have admitted it to the spunky teenager, but he did in fact have no idea of where to look. No patrol cars had called in with sightings, which meant the men were probably off the main roads already. Taking up his radio, he dispatched a car to Sisal to the west, another to Compeche, and he had his driver headed for Dzidzantún, followed closely behind by the church bus. Driving with his siren on, the two vehicle tandem wove through the afternoon traffic, hoping to arrive at their destination in time to find the boys still alive.

Inside the cave, Rick dragged Jim onto the sandy bank after swimming back to help him. He wrestled with Jim's soaked bonds, finally untying them after struggling with them for several minutes. Juan's breathing was shallow and raspy, but he was alive. Rick knew their biggest problem would be hypothermia because the cavern, which was already chilly, would become frigid very quickly after sunset.

Rick's stomach began to growl from hunger, adding yet another problem to their situation. The sound seemed to be amplified by the limestone walls. Juan smiled and nodded weakly, while Jim voiced an agreement. Having been abducted before lunch, all three were experiencing the early pangs of hunger. What concerned Rick the most was what little warmth the sunlight had already provided was quickly dissipating with the approaching night. Even if they stayed out of the water, he knew the temperatures would drop to an uncomfortable level before the morning. As the last vestiges of sunlight left the cave, Juan sat up, bracing his back against the cave's wall in order to remain upright. The boys huddled together, gathering warmth from their close proximity, temporarily stalling any attacks of fear and despair. Rick suggested they sing something, hoping to keep their spirits up, but Jim declined. Juan, whose voice sounded otherworldly in the dimness of the cave lighting, confessed that he had never really enjoyed singing church music.

"Why is that?" Rick asked.

"I do not know. Part of it is my feelings about my father. It is hard to explain. You see him as the man of God, but the truth is he does not much care about me. Everything to him is church, church, church. I love him, but I fear he does not love me."

"That's not true," Rick answered. "You should have heard him the other day in the gym. I know he spends time with the other boxers, but you're the one that he boasts about the most."

"Really?" Juan asked, sounding truly surprised.

"Sure," Jim said, supporting Rick's assessment, "but he also told us about how concerned he was that you have never accepted the Lord."

Silence followed. The lack of sound echoed ominously in the grotto. Breaking the stillness, Juan replied, "I do not know. I really do love my father, but we just have never been able to communicate," Juan said.

"Dude, that's called life," Rick said. "My father and me are close, but there are still things we can't talk about. There are times when I'm pretty sure he thinks I'm an alien."

"I remember the first time he talked about your group coming down," Juan explained, "I resented you and Jim. It was like his work with the other boxers all over again. I felt as if he was ignoring me and pushing me away. I know I treated you guys badly, especially you, Rick, and I am sorry."

In the dimness of the cavern, Rick felt the other boy's sincerity and was embarrassed that he couldn't find the words to respond. He also felt guilt for the way he had resented Juan's attention to Wendy.

"What about the Lord, Juan?"

"I love the Lord too, in my own way. I am sorry that I have never helped my father win anyone to Christ. It is funny, but when I was younger, that was all I dreamed about; him and me working together."

The sunlight was totally gone now, plunging the boys into absolute darkness. Rick felt like he was in a damp dungeon. No one knew where they were. Help was not coming and they were on their own, leaving Rick to wrestle with the reality of the futility of their situation.

"Juan, you can still make a decision for God. It's never too late to accept Jesus." Rick could no longer see the teenager's face, but he sensed his words had found their target.

Juan moved slightly, sitting up a little higher. "Rick, I do not wish to accept the Lord now, when it seems like we are going to die. That is not how I wanted to do it."

"You don't accept the Lord to die for him; you choose to live for Him. I understand the conditions aren't the best, but God understands that more than we do. The funny thing is, I never read in the Bible that grace knew anything about conditions. Besides, let's not give up hope, because I believe that God can still perform a miracle. And even if He doesn't, He's still God."

Juan began crying softly. Rick knew it wasn't out of fear, but because he felt the Lord's presence. Rick led him in prayer, and after they were done, Juan cried some more, out of a thankful heart. The other two joined him in rejoicing.

Rick surveyed the darkness. Suddenly all fear of his watery tomb was not as threatening, and the chilly air of the cavern had lost its bite, as Rick was warmed by the knowledge that somewhere angels were rejoicing.

Lieutenant Gonzalez stopped his car in the middle of the field. As far as he could see in the waning light, there was nothing but tall overgrown grass. The church van stopped directly behind the policeman's cruiser. The headlights showed where another car had recently crushed the grass. Ken immediately jumped out and began running toward the tree lines that separated the open field from the jungle.

"Please, señor," Gonzalez said. "Do not run out here. The grass is thick, and the light has gone. We need to stick together."

"But look, this part is pushed down. Another car was here and not too long ago."

Ken continued to run ahead but slowed down so the others could catch up with him.

"Where are you going?" Gonzalez demanded.

"To the northeast corner of this field. You'll find there are six cenotes in this area. I need to see the one nearest the northeast corner. If they're here, that's where they'll be."

"How do you know?" Ted asked.

Ken thought about his pattern of logic and how to explain it. "Rocky has been studying the land purchases of a former Mayor of Mérida and later Governor of the Yucatan. Land was purchased over a period of two years. It was sold or donated over a period of fifteen more years. Since Rocky stole the ledgers of the last six months of 1604, we don't know of all the land that he owned, but this plot we know was donated back to the government in 1611.

"There were three land grants where the original purchases were not recorded in any of the other ledgers. That means they must have been purchased during that six-month period. This is one of those plots."

Lieutenant Gonzalez stopped. "Okay, why do you think this Rocky character would have to come to one of those three areas?"

"Because those three parcels have not been developed yet, and if I'm right, there will be a cenote right over there, and it would surprise me if we *didn't* find them in there."

"Why do you say that?" Pastor Jiménez said.

Ken said, "You see, sir, in the jungle when they led that jaguar to our tent, they didn't care if anyone got hurt. They didn't need Rick, or Jim, or Raúl to lead them to the treasure. They just needed them to stay out of the way. The log that Rick found said the cenote was in the northeast corner of the field. I believe Rocky or León overheard them talking about it. He naturally thought it was talking about Superstition Cove as well, but it was written seven months after Sanchez left the cove. Sanchez had removed the treasure and then recorded it in the log."

"But why this area?" Gonzalez asked, barely keeping the irritation out of his voice.

"Rocky must have checked out all the other areas. He chose this one by the process of elimination. The reason I chose the three locations is because I believe Rocky wanted to rub our faces in it."

"What does it mean, rubbing our faces in it?" Gonzalez inquired.

"Rocky wants to make a statement. What a perfect way; disposing of his worst pests in the very place where he thought the treasure would be, but he had failed to find."

"I do not understand," said Raúl overhearing Ken. "You do not think the treasure is here? Why?"

Ken gave him a cryptic smile and said, "I'll show you." He led them to a flat section of the field. Gonzalez turned on a flashlight. They slowed as they neared the edge of the cenote. Kneeling beside the opening, Ken began yelling into the black void.

"RICK. JIM. JUAN. ARE YOU IN THERE?"

They listened to Ken's voice echo off the walls for several seconds, followed by ten seconds of silence. Ken was about to yell again when they finally heard a weak voice call back, "We're in here."

Chapter Nineteen

New Identities

It took two hours for the emergency team to arrive from Mérida and set up a rescue operation. Ken kept speaking encouragement to the three friends trapped inside the cave, a difficult task as Juan kept drifting in and out of consciousness. Because of the location from the cave's entrance to the sand barge where the teens were, rescuers from *el departmento de la policía del Mérida* were lowered into the cenote. Wearing thermal wet suits, their job was to assist Juan and the boys into harnesses for hauling up. Using small rubber rafts, they lifted Juan first, moving him under the opening. Jim was taken next, and then Rick. Upon clearing the mouth of the grotto, Rick immediately ran to Ted to report the activities of Rocky and León.

"The police are already aware of those two," Ted said. "We received word about twenty minutes ago that both men have been apprehended. Rocky was attempting to fly out of Mérida and León was captured in Quintana Roo. It seems they thought if they split up they would stand a better chance of escaping. By the way, León's real name is Miguel Rodriguez, and he's wanted for extortion and the murder of a police officer. Both are being detained for questioning. How are you feeling?"

Rick looked up sheepishly. "Tired, I guess." He lowered his head and stared at his soaked tennis shoes. "It looks like I sort of messed things up again."

Ted chuckled. "I wouldn't have expected less, but like usual, even your screw-ups turn out alright. Juan and his father are rejoicing right now. When Juan was conscious, the first words out of his mouth were he accepted the Lord. They're on their way to the hospital, but don't worry, it's just routine. He'll be okay. Juan owes his life to you, both spiritually and physically."

Kenny arrived and stood next to Ted, waiting to talk to Rick. Rick noticed him and said, "Ken. Thank God you were here. We owe you our lives."

The two boys embraced. Ken asked, "How does it feel to be that close to the treasure, but unable to reach it?"

Puzzled, Rick stepped back and asked, "What do you mean?"

Ken laughed and pointed to the cenote. "Remember Sanchez began selling his assets? I think it's because he hid the remainder of his treasure in that cenote."

"Wait a minute," Rick said. "Why would he hide it in water?"

Ken laughed again, as if he had just heard a funny story. "He didn't, but then he also didn't understand the nature of how grottos are formed. The Yucatan is full of these underground limestone caverns. They begin as dry openings but water gradually seeps into them, filling them up. Erosion takes place, walls are shifted, and treasure or anything else that is buried a few feet under the surface, suddenly gets covered with eighty feet of water. The treasure gets moved, sinks, or is spread out and carried by currents for miles, eventually getting re-buried or taken out to sea. No one will ever find all of that treasure. Sanchez was a man who put his confidence in hiding his treasure, and God must have been laughing at him, because God created limestone."

"Talk about building your house on the sand," Ted said laughing loudly. "Now *there's* an object lesson if ever I heard one.

Rick and Ken joined him laughing as they thought about Sanchez climbing down a hole, expecting to land on solid ground, only to get his feet wet.

Wendy and Mackenzie arrived with their host family. Wendy, spotting Rick, came running across the field.

"Rick," she screamed as she flung her arms around him and began weeping on his shoulder, "Are you alright?"

Rick was elated to see her, and he had to admit he felt better at the moment than any time since leaving his watery prison. "I'm fine, but I don't know about Jim."

Ted said, "He's being treated right now. He's over there with the rescue squad."

Rick and Wendy made their way toward the group gathered around the ambulance. Jim lay inside the vehicle on a stretcher with an oxygen mask covering his face, though it appeared that he really didn't need it and was slightly embarrassed to be laying there sucking up air. When he saw Rick and the girls, he jerked the mask off despite the pro-tests from one of the emergency workers who chased after him with a blood pressure cuff, trying to get him to return to the ambulance.

After another half hour, Lieutenant Gonzalez finished his ques-tioning and dismissed them, allowing the group to go to the hospital to check on Juan. When they arrived, they learned that Juan had been examined and the doctors all agreed that he would be fine, but they were keeping him overnight for observation due to exposure. Pastor Jiménez came down, and seeing Rick, told him that his son was asking for him.

Rick followed the minister to the third floor of the hospital. He detected the usual odors of medication and pine-scented cleansers and wondered if all hospitals smelled the same. *No wonder all the people in here are sick*, he thought to himself but resisted laughing. They walked down a long hallway that led to an intersection with three more hall-ways. They took the wing to the left and went to the third room on the right.

Juan was lying on the bed. The champion boxer looked paler than Rick could ever recall seeing him. In spite of that, he had a glow on his face that had been missing before.

In a whisper that was barely audible, Juan said, "Rick, thank you for coming."

Taking a seat beside the bed, Rick said, "It's my pleasure. Sorry how things turned out."

Juan gave a weak smile. "Thanks for helping me in the cave; first for saving my life, and second for leading me to the Lord. I will always be grateful."

"I really didn't do that much," Rick said, watching the pastor out of the corner of his eyes. "You were already hungry for God. I just helped you find Him, and if it weren't for Ken's detective skills, pulling you out of the water would have been a wasted effort."

"Not really. If we had died in that cave I would have died saved," Juan said. "Once you pulled me out of the water, everything in my life changed. I know I may not be making any sense, but…"

Juan closed his eyes, and for a minute Rick thought he had fallen asleep, but after a few seconds he reopened them. "I will be out of here tomorrow. I will see you then," he said just before he drifted off to sleep.

A special gathering took place at the Galante's ranch on Friday. A barbeque supper was catered in, with the group as the featured guests. They ate plates of chicken, pulled pork, and hamburgers with all the fixings. Everyone ate their fill, in spite of Terrell and Marcus having an eating contest with Juan and another boxer who Pastor Jiménez had just won to the Lord. While they ate, a huge bonfire was being built in the south pasture. The pastor and his wife, Juanita, were in attendance, thrilled over the conversion of their son. Both made a point to thank Rick personally. The new-found closeness of the family was evident to all, and they were joined by Ted and Brenda in their celebration. As they gathered around the bonfire, word spread that there was to be a special ceremony to honor the Ten.

Pastor Jiménez began the ceremony by thanking the group for coming to visit them in the Yucatan. This was followed by testimonies from Juan and Raúl, as they told how working with the Ten had affected them. After all the preliminaries were completed, Pastor Tate asked the Ten to step forward. As they gathered near the fire, Alfonso came walking toward them from out of the shadows wearing an Indian head-dress. Smoke from the fire danced playfully about him and encircled them all, adding an eerie quality to the evening's festivities.

"When I was a small boy of only eight years," the old Indian said, "my parents died. Even though my father was Mexican, my mother was full-blooded Apache. I was sent to the Apache reservation to be raised by my aunt and uncle. It is where I lived until I was fourteen. When I decided it was time for me to leave, they did not argue, but merely stated it was my time to take my journey into the world.

"Before I left, Chief Black Eagle gave me this headdress. Many feathers have been added through the years as they have been earned. At first, the headdress did not fit, but Black Eagle said the headdress was not meant to fit me, but rather the brave warrior that I was to become, and when the time came, my head would fit it.

"Shortly after leaving the reservation, I found the true Lord, though I have always shown my respect to Him by honoring nature and not sinning against the land. In that regard, Black Eagle would have been pleased as well.

"The Indians have a saying that you should never judge a man until you walk a day in his moccasins. That may sound familiar, and since it has been borrowed and restated in different ways, I suspect you have heard it before."

The night had grown quiet except for a bird crying out some-where beyond the firelight and a lone coyote howling at the waning moon. The wood in the fire made popping sounds, but no one said a word as they listened to the old cowhand's speech.

"We here in the Yucatan will forever be indebted to you. You have given us a new Juan, and Raúl has been affected by your presence as well. As much as you have become a part of our lives, we wish to make you forever a part of our family.

"In the Jewish culture, a child is not named until the eighth day. Names are not chosen for reasons of vanity, but to reveal a little of the child's character and identity. The Indians have a similar custom. With the Apaches, a name is given only after careful observation. Sometimes an infant is not named for several years.

"After observing you two around the ranch," he said, looking at Jim and Rick, "and after spending eight days with this group in the wilderness, I am prepared to give each of you your new names; the names that you will be remembered by."

Walking up to Monica, he placed his hands upon her shoulders. Looking into her brown eyes, he said, "Monica, you have proven your-self to be the responsible one. I have seen how you have watched over some of the other girls without smothering them or preventing them from being who they were intended to be. For this reason, you will be remembered from here on as *roble fuerte con miembros para protección.* This means 'Mighty Oak with Limbs for Protection.'"

Monica gasped, thinking of the beauty and the implications of the name. Her face radiated as she thought of the new title.

Alfonso moved to where Marcus and Terrell stood. He faced them and waited. In the darkness the coyote howled again, its cry a lonely and sad lament.

"You two have had a quiet visit, but not because you are any less important. You two offer a variety of talents and interests, and though you appear to be the same, your differences mold you and drive you in different directions. Marcus, your musical talents have been appre-ciated, but they will grow as you mature. Terrell, you have a sense of adventure and you are not afraid to face danger. Though you two are twins, God has given you different personalities. Therefore, you will be remembered as *águilas gemelas pero con plumas differentes.* That means 'Twin Eagles, but with Different Feathers.'"

Sean appeared pale in the little light emanating from the fire. Alfonso faced him.

"Sean, you seem to be lost sometimes among your older friends and their activities, however, you are simply in training to someday lead. As Timothy was to Paul, you will someday develop into leader-ship and a ministry of your own. Therefore, your memory will re-main with us and you shall be remembered as *pequeño zorro que sigue la manada quete*, or 'Little Fox Who Follows the Pack.'"

Alfonso turned robotically, crossing to where Kim and Ken stood watching the ceremony.

"Never have I seen children as smart as you two. I am sure you are both a source of pride and challenge to your parents." He paused as several members of the group giggled. "I feel privileged and honored to have met you both. You can become whatever you wish to be, and I am sure whatever it is, you will be successful at it, but it will not sur-prise those who know you that someday you will pursue endeavors, not just for personal gain, but ones that will further the Kingdom of God. For this reason, I call you, young lady, *'el buho sabio que no vuela.'* This means 'The Wise Owl that does not Fly,' and your brother will be *el lobo astuto que vive en las sombras.* That means 'The Cunning Wolf Who Dwells in the Shadows.'"

He slowly approached the last four. The wrinkles in his face ap-peared like tiny crevices, accented by the dancing light of the camp-fire. He looked at Mackenzie and Wendy and said, "You two are both most lovely, and a pleasure to watch even with my ancient eyes. My eyes have viewed many women of great beauty, but I can see in both of you an inner quality as well. To us, Mackenzie, you will be proclaimed as *la flor tranquila que todo lo ve;* 'Quiet Flower that sees all.'

"Miss Wendy, please be honored as we call you *pequeña princesa con el pelo encendido.* That means 'Little princess with the fiery hair.'"

The night seemed to come to total silence as Alfonso turned and stopped directly in front of Jim and Rick.

Chapter Twenty

Home, Home from the Range

Jim had stood mesmerized as the old warrior prophesied over the others. He felt both pride at being a part of the ceremony, and shame, because he felt inadequate at the moment. He felt he hadn't really done anything. As before, he had followed Rick as his friend plunged headlong into their latest adventure. Even in the grotto, it had been Rick who saved Juan and him from drowning and led Juan to the Lord. He felt he hadn't done anything worthy of honor.

"*Señor* Jim," Alfonso said as he approached the last two members. "Meeting you has given my old heart a joy that it has not felt in years. Like me, you have mastered the most difficult job on the reservation. You have learned how to play the second tom-tom. You have found pleasure in helping rather than leading. It is because of that, that God will, in time, give you both the chance to help and to lead. Your new name shall be *al amigo leal que cuida de*, or 'Loyal friend who keeps watch.'"

As Alfonso faced Rick, the fire popped again and an owl hooted. Sparks flew in the dark air and disappeared like dying fireflies. The night seemed to smother Rick like a blanket, creating a surrealistic atmosphere, insulating him from all sense of reality. It seemed as if time had stopped, with the only movement the flames lapping out at the night sky.

"Rick, you have shown great kindness to your horse Ginger. If I knew nothing else about you, that would have been enough. Still, you have a sense of adventure that leads you in many directions, and like the tumbleweed, you follow the wind and take no thought of the destination, but only the journey. The name that I have chosen for you is *el pequeño mustango con un buen corazón.* That my good friend means the little mustang with a good heart."

Rick felt a warm sensation in his heart and face. Flabbergasted at the entire ceremony, he wished secretly that he had done more. The box, with its ship's log, the dagger, and the doubloons had been donated to the museum, with a plaque honoring the Gideon Ten for their contribution. Also, Kenny's observations concerning the identity of the former mayor would be enough to keep their historians busy for months and maybe even years. The reward money received for the information that led to the capture of Miguel Rodriguez was donated and placed in a trust fund for the future education of Juan and Raúl.

Pastor Jiménez took the foreground again and led them in prayer, blessing God and thanking Him for the Ten. When he finished, it was time to call it a night. The next day the group was to fly home, and everyone knew their departure would only be symbolic, as pieces of their hearts would remain in the Yucatan for many years to come.

The group flew back on Saturday, and even though they had been up fairly late the previous night, they were eager, and in fact enthusiastic, to go home. When the plane landed and the group passed through the tunnel ramp, they were surprised to find a welcoming committee from Riverside. All their parents stood waiting for them along with Pastor Tate and a contingency of members from Riverside Life Tabernacle who had come to greet them as well. Several signs had been made and were held aloft, welcoming the group of teens back from Mexico.

Rick, Monica, and Sean hugged their parents, and gave the mandatory attention to Julie, who made them kiss her teddy bear as well. Rick's father commented on the stories he had been told about their exploits, and while he intended it to be a reprimand, his voice betrayed a sense of pride.

Passing by a newspaper stand, Rick was surprised to see brightly colored flyers lying on top of the daily publication. Looking at the flyer, he saw the picture of a girl and a request for information as to her whereabouts from the F.B.I. Rick picked up one of the flyers and placed it in his backpack. As he was leaving, he looked back to see a police officer pick up the rest of the flyers and carry them away.

The group was just getting ready to gather their luggage when two men came rushing up to them. It was Detective Smallwood with a uniformed Sam Upton trailing close behind.

"I was hoping to get here before you all took off for home," the hard-faced detective said. "We wanted to greet the group and welcome them back."

Looking at Rick and Jim he added, "I heard you two failed to take my advice about staying out of trouble."

Rick could not tell if he was joking or not, as the detective's face remained solemn and noncommittal. Wondering if he would ever hear the end of it Rick answered, "It just sort of happened."

"Well, I spoke to Lieutenant Gonzalez of the Mérida Police Department and he told me the two men should do some major time for attempted murder and kidnapping, not to mention that Rocky has been a suspect for smuggling Mayan artifacts out of the country for quite some time. The man who called himself León will be in prison even longer for murder. You guys tangled with some pretty tough characters. We'll have to talk some more about it later, but meanwhile, welcome back."

During the week and a half prior to the start of school, the Ten were busy doing extra chores and serving out their restrictions that they had earned before leaving for the Yucatan. As incredible as it seemed, they all looked forward to school as a chance to get out of their houses; none more than Rick.

Rick was pleased to find Wendy and Jim had been assigned to his homeroom. Many of their school friends had heard about their adventures in the Yucatan and wanted to hear all about it. Many of them were even amazed when they learned of the group's involvement in capturing the burglars that had been operating in Riverside. The newspaper accounts had left their names out of the articles. It seemed almost, to Rick, like they had reached celebrity status overnight. Not accustomed to notoriety, the sensation made him feel slightly uncomfortable.

The first day of classes was slow, consisting mostly of receiving schedules, books, seating assignments, and lab partners. Still, seventh period was one class that Rick looked forward to. He had signed up for Spanish I to meet his Foreign Language requirements, but now hoped he could learn enough to correspond with Juan and Raúl. Before leaving, they had made the two teens from the Yucatan honorary members of the Gideon Ten. They also made Bob Browning, catcher on the Bulldogs baseball team, the eleventh member upon arriving home.

As Rick took his seat in Spanish class, he felt a tap on his shoulder. He was surprised when he turned to find Wendy sitting behind him.

"I thought you were going to take French?" he said.

"I was, but four weeks in the Yucatan has spoiled me for any other language, so I changed my schedule. Besides, you think I want to risk you having some other girl as a study partner?"

Rick smiled, praying she was only kidding.

The teacher's name was Mrs. Springer, a slimly built, middle-aged woman in her third year at Riverside Middle School. As she sat, she surveyed the room full of new faces and smiled. The first thing she did was have one of the students pass out the books. Standing before the class she said, "I want to teach you how to introduce yourselves in Spanish. There are two acceptable ways. The first is *me llamo* Betty Springer, which means I call myself Betty Singer. The other is *mi nombre es* Betty Springer, which translates my name is Betty Springer. Now let's try it together."

She led the room in the simple exercise, and then, one by one, she had them introduce themselves. Each student stood and gave their names, sat down, and the next one stood and repeated the action.

When it came her turn, Wendy stood and said, "*Mi nombre es* Wendy Patterson." She sat down and looked at Rick.

Rick reflected on the summer and all that had transpired. He thought of Randy Hinkle and Luke Fairley in jail awaiting trial and, ultimately, sentencing. Then he thought of Rocky and León on their way to a Mexican prison. He thought of the Bulldog's championship, the jaguar attack, eight hours trapped in a grotto, and half a dozen new believers. Alfonso was right. Rick was wild at times, but how did Ted put it? *How is it you keep getting into so much trouble, when all you're really trying to do is the right thing?*

They were all correct, but good came out of his recklessness and the Lord received the praise in the end. All those thoughts raced through his head. He reflected on the last night when Alphonso gave them all new names. What was it the old Indian called him? The little mustang with a good heart. Finally, as if it came in one humongous epiphany, Rick stood, faced the class, and delivered the only response he thought appropriate.

"*Me llamo es pequeño mustango con un buen corazón.*"

Baseball Trivia

As mentioned in the story, there are eight ways a player can reach first base without getting a hit according to official baseball rules.

1. Base on balls/walk
2. Hit by pitch
3. Error
4. Fielder's choice
5. Catcher interference
6. Third strike not caught
7. Batted ball hits an umpire or runner before contact with a fielder

The eighth way is often overlooked by people, even if they Googled it for a response. The eighth and final answer is:

8. Pinch runner

Acknowledgements

Special thanks to the team at Outskirts Press under the supervision of Bridget Horstmann and Justene Presley. Their talented staff brought my first book to life in ways that I could never have imagined. Also to Lisa Jones who oversaw the production of this installment of the Gideon Ten series.

Also thanks to my sister, Wanda Davis, and my good friend, Loretta Landon, for reading my manuscripts and offering their advice and editing skills. To my son, Joshua, for listening to me read the manuscript. He hears things that I often overlook while writing my stories. His input has proved to be invaluable.

Lastly, special thanks to Janice Luciano and Ramone Flores, two of my coworkers, for correcting my horrible Spanish. After four quarters at The Ohio State University, I know just enough to get myself mugged in Miami.

Lastly, for my friends who supported my first book and gave me positive feedback, I thank them as well. Their kind words and messages of encouragement made it possible for me to continue. If my writings are a blessing to anyone, then rewards in Heaven must be shared with them as well.

www.ingramcontent.com/pod-product-compliance
Lightning Source LLC
Chambersburg PA
CBHW052105090426
42741CB00009B/1686